CAMBRIDGE LIBRARY COLLECTION

Books of enduring scholarly value

Travel and Exploration

The history of travel writing dates back to the Bible, Caesar, the Vikings and the Crusaders, and its many themes include war, trade, science and recreation. Explorers from Columbus to Cook charted lands not previously visited by Western travellers, and were followed by merchants, missionaries, and colonists, who wrote accounts of their experiences. The development of steam power in the nineteenth century provided opportunities for increasing numbers of 'ordinary' people to travel further, more economically, and more safely, and resulted in great enthusiasm for travel writing among the reading public. Works included in this series range from first-hand descriptions of previously unrecorded places, to literary accounts of the strange habits of foreigners, to examples of the burgeoning numbers of guidebooks produced to satisfy the needs of a new kind of traveller - the tourist.

The Love-life of Dr Kane

Elisha Kane (1820–57) was a famous U.S. Arctic explorer who fell in love with the well-known New York spiritualist Margaret Fox (1836–93). When their secret engagement was revealed, it caused much controversy and Fox was later accused of fabricating their subsequent marriage. She wanted to publish their correspondence in 1862 to clear her name, but Kane's family – who disapproved of Fox and did not believe the couple ever married – halted the book's publication and they reached a settlement. When they failed to make agreed payments to Fox, she decided to publish the letters in 1866. The subsequent volume charts the couple's courtship from its beginnings in 1852 until Kane's death, and reveals the ups and downs of their tumultuous relationship, especially Kane's desire for Fox to stop her spiritualist practices. It presents an intimate account of the romance between two prominent nineteenth-century public figures.

T0352082

Cambridge University Press has long been a pioneer in the reissuing of out-of-print titles from its own backlist, producing digital reprints of books that are still sought after by scholars and students but could not be reprinted economically using traditional technology. The Cambridge Library Collection extends this activity to a wider range of books which are still of importance to researchers and professionals, either for the source material they contain, or as landmarks in the history of their academic discipline.

Drawing from the world-renowned collections in the Cambridge University Library and other partner libraries, and guided by the advice of experts in each subject area, Cambridge University Press is using state-of-the-art scanning machines in its own Printing House to capture the content of each book selected for inclusion. The files are processed to give a consistently clear, crisp image, and the books finished to the high quality standard for which the Press is recognised around the world. The latest print-on-demand technology ensures that the books will remain available indefinitely, and that orders for single or multiple copies can quickly be supplied.

The Cambridge Library Collection brings back to life books of enduring scholarly value (including out-of-copyright works originally issued by other publishers) across a wide range of disciplines in the humanities and social sciences and in science and technology.

The Love-life of Dr Kane

Containing the Correspondence,
and a History of the Acquaintance,
Engagement, and Secret Marriage
Between Elisha K. Kane and Margaret Fox

ANONYMOUS

CAMBRIDGE
UNIVERSITY PRESS

CAMBRIDGE UNIVERSITY PRESS

Cambridge, New York, Melbourne, Madrid, Cape Town,
Singapore, São Paolo, Delhi, Mexico City

Published in the United States of America by Cambridge University Press, New York

www.cambridge.org
Information on this title: www.cambridge.org/9781108050128

© in this compilation Cambridge University Press 2012

This edition first published 1866
This digitally printed version 2012

ISBN 978-1-108-05012-8 Paperback

MARGARET FOX KANE.

From a Portrait taken 1862.

CARLETON PUBLISHER NEW YORK.

THE

LOVE-LIFE OF DR. KANE;

CONTAINING

THE CORRESPONDENCE, AND A HISTORY OF THE
ACQUAINTANCE, ENGAGEMENT, AND
SECRET MARRIAGE BETWEEN

ELISHA K. KANE AND MARGARET FOX,

WITH FACSIMILES OF LETTERS,
AND HER PORTRAIT.

NEW YORK:
Carleton, Publisher, 413 *Broadway.*
M DCCC LXVI.

R. CRAIGHEAD,
Printer, Stereotyper, and Electrotyper,
Carton Building,
81, 83, and 85 Centre Street.

CONTENTS.

VI.

VII.

VIII.

IX.

X.

XI.

XII.

XIII.

XIV.

XV.

XVI.

XVII.

XVIII.

XIX.

XX.

XXI

XXII.

XXIII.

PREFACE.

It is customary, in publishing personal memoirs or private correspondence, to make some apology for presenting to the world that which was never intended to meet the public eye. In the case of love-letters this seems especially necessary, if one would avoid the imputation of want of delicacy. Perhaps many will think that no circumstances could justify the publication of the letters contained in this volume. But, after long consideration, those whose opinions are entitled to respect, have judged differently. The lady to whom they were addressed has ever held these letters as too sacred for any eyes save her own to rest upon. She has borne poverty and privation, when their publication many years ago might have given her an independence; and that, too, notwithstanding that the small sum left in trust for her by Dr. Kane has been (except the interest for a time) withheld from her. She has borne the sneers of the world, and the neglect of those whose regard for the deceased should have induced them to protect, comfort, and befriend her. She has borne most injurious calumnies, which from time to time have reached her in her seclusion. Those slanders against her fair name have been repeated in various publications; yet she might be willing to receive in silence even this bitterest portion of her cup of sorrow, and go down to the grave covered with unjust obloquy, were the choice left entirely to herself. But it has not been so left. After repeated threats that Dr. Kane's letters (her only treasure and vindication) could and would be taken from her by process of law, she reluctantly consented to have copies of them made. After this was done, the judgment of friends overruled her objections, and the letters were incorporated in a memoir. Their publication, it was urged, would vindicate the honor of *both* parties to the correspondence; for *both* had severely suffered from the slanders spread abroad.

In 1862, the volume was in press; but its publication, as well as a suit in the Orphans' court, Philadelphia, for dower, on the widow's part, was stopped by a compromise with the brothers and executor of Dr. Kane. One of the brothers agreed to pay her an annuity equal to the interest of the money left her, in quarterly instalments, and the sum of two thousand dollars down, to repay the expenses she had incurred, provided she would discontinue the suit for dower, and would seal up the letters and copies, with the MS. memoir, proof-sheets, &c., and place them in the hands of a Trustee, who should be bound to prevent her access to them, and to surrender them to the Kane family at her death. The Trustee selected was Dr. Edward Bayard, of New York. A bond was executed by the brother aforesaid, for the faithful performance of the stipulated terms. In the event of the failure to pay any quarterly instalment of the annuity, Mrs. Kane was permitted to reclaim her letters, &c., from the Trustee. This agreement was soon violated by the refusal of the brother of the late Dr. Kane, to pay more than one half the sum named in his bond for her expenses. A demand was made on his part that she should release him from this obligation, which, in justice to those to whom she was indebted, she could not do. For the sake of others who had trusted her, she was compelled to resort to another suit in hopes of obtaining the remaining half of the promised sum; but she was unable to afford the expense necessary to carry it on, or to encounter the " legal dodges " and delays resorted to by the defendant to evade the fulfilment of the conditions of his bond. Then her quarterly payments of annuity—which she had regarded as strictly her own—the interest of money bequeathed to her—a mere pittance, insufficient of itself for the humblest maintenance *—were withheld from time to time, till she was forced to repeated applications and solicitations therefor. Threats were made of refusing payment of the annuity entirely, unless she released the thousand dollars aforesaid, and discontinued the suit to recover the same. Mortified at being compelled to receive as a grudged bounty what she was entitled to under any circumstances and without any contingencies— and worn out with the continuance of a strife so vexatious and humiliating—Mrs. Kane at length allowed matters to take their course; and when the quarterly annuity due in May, 1865, was in default, she availed

---

* It is said that the Kane family have received one hundred thousand dollars from the copyrights of the late Dr. Kane.

1*

herself of the privilege guaranteed to her by the terms
of the bond, and reclaimed her letters of the Trustee.
She declared her determination never again to part
with a treasure in which her very life was bound up.

When the fact of her marriage with the late Dr.
Kane was alluded to in the newspapers a short time
since, a telegram from Philadelphia, pronouncing "the
story" "a canard," was sent in the name of the Kane
family to the Associated Press. Could any woman who
respected herself, submit to such an indignity? What
was there about her whom Dr. Kane had wooed and
wedded, that she should be thus insulted, and denied
common justice under an outrageous imputation? Her
sole means of defence, her only vindication—was the
publication of this correspondence.

The world usually sides with the rich, the proud, and
the powerful; and it is not expected that the poor, the
humble, and the weak, will receive either justice or
sympathy. But some good will be accomplished in the
unquestionable proof afforded of the pure and spotless
character of the two persons whose hearts are laid open
in this correspondence. The publication may do service also to the community, in exhibiting the folly of
that spirit of prejudice, which in this instance helped to
cut short one valued life, and irreparably blighted another.

Several unimportant letters, and some nearly repeti-
tions of others, have been left out of the collection; and
in one or two instances, portions in which persons are
mentioned or alluded to, have been omitted. Portions
of other letters were taken out by Dr. Kane himself.

(BEFORE MARRIAGE)

And now dear Maggie, my own dear Maggie, live a life of purity and goodness. Consecrate it to me... bear no guilt upon which even the breath of an angel could leave a stain. Thus live, dear Maggie, until God brings me back to you — and then — meeting my eye with the proud consciousness of virtue — we will rejoin ourselves to a position sanctified by love and marriage. Golden fields shall spread before us their summer harvest. Silver lakes mirror your very breath. Let us live for each other — Farewell!

E. K. KANE.

(AFTER MARRIAGE)

Dear Wife — May I meet you at half past ten to night. I have a capital excuse for good Mother. Do not say no but send word the earliest hour and I'll be with you.

I thank you, dear Maggie, for your kind letter. I have rode in this cold wind nearly eighteen miles but this afternoon shall see me in your company.

What say you to tomorrow for one holyday! — all your own.

Do not be afraid of thinking too much of me. For even if the dear old Polar Winter should make me a perpetual smile, the memory of a dead affection would be better than a recollected coolness.

If you think me afraid of letters here is my contradiction.

E. N. KANE!

U. S. Navy!!
No 35 Juneal St!!
Philad.a !!!!!

Miss Margaret Fox
Philad.a

The material originally positioned here is too large for reproduction in this reissue. A PDF can be downloaded from the web address given on page iv of this book, by clicking on 'Resources Available'.

INTRODUCTION.

A REVIEWER of Dr. Elder's Biography of Dr. E. K. Kane, noticing the author's statement that he had access to the private correspondence of the great explorer, and claimed the credit of showing all the important points of his life and character—says: " It is because we are satisfied that Dr. Elder only had access to *part* of the Doctor's private correspondence, and because the book records only the exterior and gilded life of Dr. Kane, that we are obliged to look upon it as defective. There was a deep under-current in the navigator's life, which the distinguished biographer knew nothing of, and which the family did not place at his disposal. We allude to the love-life of Dr. Kane; the spontaneous feelings which produced the extensive 'private correspondence' with a young lady in New York, in which his real inner existence is manifest. The biography would have been more strictly true, if it had revealed the fact of an engagement there, in which his feelings were fully enlisted; but which he repudiated when he returned covered with the tinsel and show of glory, because his friends thought it beneath him to marry one who had not the stamp of dollars and aristocracy to add to his renown. In this his courage failed, and he yielded his own higher feelings to the vain applause of the world; while he insisted on keeping up a correspondence with the young lady after he went to Cuba, and until near the time of his death. Here is a phase of Dr. Kane's life which should be made public; and if the letters are ever published (an event not likely to occur, we learn), another important leaf can be added to the biography which has just appeared."

There is certainly no kind of correspondence that so reveals the inner life and soul of a man as his love-letters. No experience, like that of the heart, commands sympathy, because none so fully discloses and renders us intimate with the individual. The most detailed record of Dr. Kane's plans, adventures, and achievements, could not throw half the light on his personal character that a memoir of his love-life does.

The loves of eminent men, through the world's literary history, have not only shared their renown, but have aided them to deserve it. Petrarch—the model after whom the early poets shaped their amorous fancies—does not the world owe him to Laura? And does not Waller live in Saccharissa? From Wyatt and Surrey—through the poetical literature of Elizabeth and the First and Second Charles—down

to the " Grand Turk of amatory verse," Lord Byron,
and the bards of the present day, the love-element
has contributed vastly to the popularity of poetry.
It is by the story of his love for the fair Geraldine—
marvellous as a knightly romance—that the Earl of
Surrey is held in remembrance ; it is for Stella's sake
that we linger over the sonnets of Sydney. Who
thinks of Klopstock without Meta ? And who for-
gets the tender sadness that breathes in Donne's complaints, in his laconic epistle—" John Donne—Anne
Donne—undone ! " The loves of Burns—numberless
as leaves in Vallambrosa, or " the gay motes that
people the sunbeams,"—what would his poetry be
without them ?

Letters between lovers are still more interesting,
because they bring the actual life and feelings of the
writers closer to our sympathies. The letters of
Stella and Vanessa to Swift have embalmed their
names. How many have sighed over the tender sorrows of Abelard and Heloise ! The correspondence
of Goethe with Bettina will live as long as the most
elaborate works of the great poet.

The letters of love and friendship of a man of
science and heroic adventure are the more valuable
as they form almost the only outlet for his proper
individuality. The learned man or the hero, in such
outpourings of his secret heart, appears in an aspect
contrasted with that of his public life, and the more
affecting in proportion to the contrast. Thus we

become convinced—to use the language of the biographer of Dr. Kane—that "our man of mighty enterprise and world-wide notoriety had a heart and soul in him; all nerve to the demands of duty, but in the deepest, dearest sense, all tenderness, devotion, and tact in the offices of affection."

The brief and brilliant career of Dr. Kane was marked by more of both suffering and achievement than has been crowded into the history of as few years in the lives of the most remarkable men. It has been well said that "no human quantity of omniscience and providence would have been a full match for the duties with which this one man was burdened." When we see the man thus pressed under his multitudinous obligations—"while his pen was running, his telegraphs flying,"—while "he was worrying the Department, examining recruits, inventing cooking-stoves, pricing rounds of beef, rummaging the Medical Bureau at Washington—till he had succeeded in begging some two thousand dollars' worth of outfit, all the while up to his elbows in a batch of Department dough, that was only souring while he was trying to make it rise,"—when we see him at a milliner's choosing a little girl's bonnet, trying to catch an escaped canary bird in Philadelphia, or quitting his work on the very eve of embarking upon his great expedition, to go over a hundred miles to comfort a homesick schoolgirl in her country seclusion —we are all the more touched by his tenderness, and

wonder at the depth and ardor of the love that
impelled him. So the little incident of his carrying
the portrait of his beloved one strapped to his back,
through the dreary Arctic wastes, gives us a better
insight into a true and noble heart than all the anec-
dotes collated by his biographer.

There was a complication in this attachment of
Dr. Kane's which does not belong to ordinary love
affairs. The young girl to whom his heart was
given, whom he so often called his "godsend," was
inferior to him in social position. This may sound
strangely in America, where, in theory, no social
distinctions are recognised, and where ability and
education every day elevate their possessor to superior power and influence in spite of difficulties. But
it was not want of fortune nor want of education
that *alone* stood in the way. The profession of
mediumship for "spiritual manifestations" was from
its commencement under the ban of public disfavor
and suspicion. It was generally supposed that
deception was practised on the credulous by artful
persons who made money out of the delusions they
created. That one so distinguished and highly
esteemed as Dr. Kane should love and wed an
untutored girl, with only beauty and virtue for her
dower, was scarcely pardonable by a proud family;
but the added odium of the spirit-rapping association
his family could not possibly bear; his friends shrank
from it; he, himself, with all his tried bravery, trem-

bled to encounter it. This dread of public derision, of the censure and pity of those he esteemed, of the lowering which his reputation might suffer, caused the struggles apparent in many of his earlier letters, between his regard for the world's opinion and the love that had entwined itself with every fibre of his being. How deep and strong must that love have been, to come off victorious from such a conflict!

His affection was not strengthened in its first growth by any fervent response from its fair object. She was in years almost a child, in experience wholly one; surrounded by the disciples of spiritualism, who regarded her as a chosen apostle of the new belief, and by kindred most unwilling to give her up to a destiny that would remove her far from them. There was opposition, rather than favor, among her nearest relations, to the suit of her lover. She was proud, too, in her gentle way, and perhaps not disposed to open her maiden heart unreservedly to one who despised her associates, condemned her calling, and often thought himself bound in self-respect to give her up for ever. The consciousness of his own superiority seemed ever present, even in the warmest expressions of his regard; and she was too young to perceive in this unwilling condescension the strongest proof of the power of her own attractions. This state of things should be borne in mind while reading letters that appear strange on the Doctor's side, or cold and reserved on hers. It was, in Dr. Kane's

own words, " a mutual dread " that trammelled both;
—this.fear of the censures and the misconstruction
of those around them.   Never was a " course of true
love " pursued under circumstances more unpro-
pitious.

In both, the affection proved strong enough to
triumph over adverse circumstances.   The young
girl abjured " the spirits " for ever; suffered herself
to be separated from kindred and early associations,
and gave herself irrevocably in a life-consecration to
the chosen of her heart.   Her coldness was changed
to a devotion which death itself has had no power to
chill or destroy.   The lover, after a severe conflict
with the tyranny of Prejudice—that absolute sove-
reign of the American republic—returned to his
allegiance to his soul's first and only idol.   Faithful
to death was he, and the victory thus gained in the
strength of a noble nature, does him as much honor
as any achieved under the banner of science.

The account given by Smucker in his Life of Dr.
Kane, is incorrect in the statement that the engagement of Miss Fox and Dr. Kane commenced before
the Doctor's first Arctic Expedition.   It was shortly
before his last one.   Nor could the young lady be
considered as of " inferior " birth.   Her father was a
reputable and well-to-do farmer, who owned a fine
estate in Canada, where Margaret was born, and con-
siderable property in the western part of the State
of New York.   His ancestors were highly respectable

Germans, the name being originally Voss. Mrs. Fox was of the Rutan family, of French origin, and of ancient and honorable lineage. Some of her relations of that name still reside near Montreal, possessors of a magnificent estate, and esteemed among the wealthy aristocracy of the country. Mr. Fox unfortunately lost his excellent Canadian property, but retained a small farm in New York. He and his wife were members of the Methodist church in good standing, and were always respected by their neighbors.

MEMOIR.

I.

LATE in the autumn of 1852, Mrs. Fox and her daughter Margaret were occupying rooms at Webb's Union Hotel, in Arch Street, Philadelphia, for the purpose of giving receptions to those who wished to investigate the phenomena of what was called "Spiritual Manifestations." Some years had elapsed since this marvel had originated in the famous "Rochester knockings," in the family of Mr. Fox. Public attention had been drawn to the strange occurrences which were reported in the newspapers; committees of inquiry had visited the house of Mr. Fox, and had conversed and tried experiments with the little girls in whose presence the sounds were heard. No one could penetrate the acknowledged mystery; although, when exhibitions were given in New York, many gentlemen distinguished for scientific attainments had examined the matter repeatedly. The attention drawn to it spread rapidly throughout the United States and throughout the world. Invitations to visit the principal cities poured upon the family, sometimes half-a-dozen telegraphic despatches being received in a day. In compliance with these urgent and importunate requests to allow the curious an opportunity of investigation, the mother of the youthful but already celebrated "mediums" determined to make a short sojourn in Philadelphia and Washington before taking up her residence in New York.

It is at all times easy to create a sensation in Philadelphia. The number of Quakers who live there, the social habits of the people, the absence of public amusements generally patronized, render the population—especially the higher and more educated part of it—peculiarly susceptible to any excitement stirring their neighborhood or their quiet city. Such a wonder as "spirit-rappings" would naturally cause a prodigious commotion. It is not surprising that the receptions were thronged, and that the "medium" and the "manifestations" were the subject of general comment. Mrs. Fox had left her youngest daughter, Katharine, then a mere child, at school in New York; and Margaret, then scarcely thirteen years of age, was the one through whom "the spirits" held converse with those of this world who sought communication with their ghostships. The rappings made in her presence were startlingly loud, and the invisible agents seemed to derive great power from her organization to make their various demonstrations. She herself never had looked deeply enough into the mystery to have any belief at all as to the phenomena.

The most prominent and fashionable people of the city came to hear the mysterious "knockings," and to have their questions answered. Clergymen and doctors, scientific and literary persons, the lovely and the learned, the sentimental and the stern, were daily in attendance; and yet the wonder grew.

One morning, about ten o'clock, Dr. E. K. Kane entered the magnificent "bridal parlors" which were appropriated to the spiritual sittings. It was his first visit; and, seeing a very young lady sitting by the window with a book in her hand, he imagined that he had knocked at the wrong door. "I beg your pardon, madam," he said in a low voice to Mrs. Fox, "I have made some mistake; can you direct me to the rooms where the 'spiritual manifestations' are shown?"

The lady informed him he was not mistaken, and invited him to take a seat at the table, to which the youthful medium was presently summoned.

The Doctor paid little attention, however, to the spirits. He entered into conversation with Mrs. Fox, now and then glancing at Margaret, who still held the book of French exercises she had been studying, and by stealth read the lesson whenever the conversation permitted. She was intent on her studies, and little dreamed that the gentleman she now saw for the first time would exercise such an influence over her future destinies.

Dr. Kane afterwards said repeatedly that his deter-

mination was formed on this first interview to make
Margaret his wife. Little as she suspected his feelings, he loved her at first sight. Her beauty was of
that delicate kind which grows on the heart, rather
than captivates the sense at a glance; she possessed
in a high degree that retiring modesty which shuns
rather than seeks admiration. The position in which
she was placed imposed on her unusual reserve and
self-control, and an ordinary observer might not have
seen in her aught to make a sudden impression. But
there was more than beauty in the charm about her
discerned by the penetrating eyes of her new
acquaintance. The winning grace of her modest
demeanor, and the native refinement apparent in
every look and movement, word and tone, were evidences of a nature enriched with all the qualities that
dignify and adorn womanhood; of a soul far above
her present calling, and those who surrounded her.
To appreciate her real superiority, her age and the
circumstances must be considered. She was yet a
little child—untutored, except in the elements of
instruction to be gained in country district schools,
when it was discovered that she possessed a mysterious power, for which no science or theory could
account. This brought her at once into notoriety,
and gathered around her those who had a fancy for
the supernatural, and who loved to excite the wonder
of strangers. Most little girls would have been
spoiled by that kind of attention. The endurance

of it without having her head turned, argued rare delicacy, simplicity, and firmness of character. After exhibitions given in different cities, to find herself an object of public attention, and of flattering notice from persons of distinction, would naturally please the vanity of a beautiful young girl; and it would not be surprising if a degree of self-conceit were engendered. But Margaret was not vain, and could not be made self-conceited. If she had any consciousness of her exquisite loveliness,—if it pleased her to possess pretty dresses and ornaments—her delight was that of a happy child taking pleasure in beautiful things without reference to any effect they might enable her to produce. Perhaps no young girl ever lived more free from the least idea of coquetry or conquest. She heeded not the expressions of admiration that reached her ear so frequently. She had seen enough of the world at this time to be aware of the advantages of a superior education, and it was the most ardent wish of her heart to make herself a well educated woman. Thus every moment she could spare was devoted to study. She never appeared in public without some older lady, and in the sittings was invariably accompanied by her mother. Young as she was, and thus secluded from familiar approach, it is not likely she had ever thought of beaux, or the admiration of the other sex.

When Dr. Kane had left the rooms on the occasion

just mentioned, Miss Fox expressed herself pleased
with his manners and conversation. The next day
he came again. This time he took little or no heed
of the spirits, but addressed his conversation to the
young lady, and spoke seriously to her of the course
she was pursuing. "This is no life for you, my
child," he said, plainly. He pointed out the dangers
of living so continually in the public eye, especially
to one so young. "You ought to go to school and
remain there some years, till your education is completed," he continued. His words found an echo in
Margaret's own wishes, and she listened to him with
still increasing respect and attention. She had, in
fact, no pleasure in her professional life, and could
not but perceive that she was regarded by many
with distrust, and that others openly charged her
with deception, supposing that she had some occult
machinery for making the raps, and for answering
the queries of the deluded. Poor girl! with her
simplicity, ingenuousness, and timidity, she could
not, had she been so inclined, have practised the
slightest deception with any chance of success.

Dr. Kane became a daily visitor, and sometimes
came twice or thrice a day; introducing many of his
friends and relatives to the wonderful rappings—
much as in his heart he disliked them—for the opportunity they afforded him of seeing and talking with
the fair young priestess of those mysteries. One day,
when there was a "circle," he wrote on a slip of

paper and handed to her the question—"Were you ever in love?"

The young lady blushed, and wrote her reply, playfully bidding him "ask the spirits."

Notes like the following, received every day, testified that the writer kept her in mind.

[Dr. Kane to Mrs. Fox.]

"Dr. Kane will call at three o'clock P.M., for the purpose of accompanying Mrs. and Miss Fox upon an afternoon drive.

"RENSSELAER, Dec. 7th, 1852."

———

[Dr. Kane to Miss Fox.]

"Dr. Kane leaves for New York on Monday; might he ask Miss Fox at what hour she would be disengaged before his departure?

"GIRARD STREET, Dec. 10th, 1852."

———

[Dr. Kane to Miss Fox.]

"MY DEAR MISS FOX:—The day is so beautiful that I feel tempted to repent my indoor imprisonment. If you will do me the kindness to change your own mind, and take a quiet drive, I will call for you at your own hour.

"With respect, very faithfully your servant,

"E. K. KANE.

"PHILA., Dec. 12th, 1852."

————

In the following note to Mrs. Fox, Dr. Kane refers to Miss Katharine Fox, then at school in New York, and residing with a lady medium—a relative, whose "establishment" for spiritual manifestations was in Twenty-sixth Street:

[Dr. Kane to Mrs. Fox.]

"MY DEAR MADAM :—I left New York this morning, and return again to-morrow. If you have any messages to send to your daughter, I should be happy to convey them, as I take a large party of my lady friends on Saturday to her establishment.

"I will call between five and six o'clock this afternoon.

"I could not resist the temptation of sending the accompanying little trifle of ermine, for Miss Margaretta's throat. As I know you to be carefully fastidious as to forms, permit me to place it in your hands.

"Pray pardon the pocket-worn condition of the enclosed note.

"Very faithfully your ob't serv't,

"E. K. KANE.

"GIRARD STREET, Dec. 18th, 1852."

———

Not very long after his first visit, Dr. Kane brought his favorite cousin, Mrs. Patterson—a very lovely woman—to see Miss Fox. A day or two afterwards Mrs. Fox received this note.

[Dr. Kane to Mrs. Fox.]

"MY DEAR MADAM :—The day is so beautiful that I will call with Mrs. Patterson, at half-past two, in hopes of persuading Miss Margaret to take the vacant place in her carriage.

"Tell Miss Maggie to dress warmly.

"Faithfully your ob't serv'nt,

"E. K. KANE.

"MRS. FOX."

These are but few notes among very many of the same kind.

One day while sitting near the table where there was a circle, Dr. Kane wrote the following lines, and handed them to the young medium.

"A PROPHECY.

" Now thy long day's work is o'er,
    Fold thine arms across thy breast;
    Weary ! weary is the life
    By cold deceit oppressed.

" Thee shall harrowing care and sorrow
    Fret, while journeying to the tomb;
    Triumph lasts not till the morrow;
    Beauty shall feast the worm.
        Dreary, dreary, ever dreary,
        Sad and same—and ever weary;
        Dreary too, from night to morn,
        Thou shalt live and die forlorn."

Some time afterwards Mrs. Fox expected her youngest daughter from New York. She received the following note from Dr. Kane in relation to that young lady's expected journey.

[Dr. Kane to Mrs. Fox.]

" MY DEAR MADAM:—It has just occurred to me that your daughter would have to change from cars to steamboat at Camden or Taconey. This would not be very pleasant to a young lady unaccompanied by a friend. If, therefore, you will send me word when your telegraph arrives, I will be happy to meet

Miss Kate on the boat and give her the aid of my
escort.

" Very faithfully your ob't servant,
"E. K. KANE.

"GIRARD ST., Jan. 10th, 10 A.M.

" MRS. FOX, Philadelphia."

Such notes as the next would accompany some
little present.

[Dr. Kane to Mrs. Fox.]

" MY DEAR MADAM :—Although I am still skeptical as to our friends in the other country, I am a
firm believer in my friends in this. As such, knowing that we must soon part, I have taken the liberty
of presenting to Miss Margaret a little memento of
our short acquaintance. May I ask you to accept
also of the accompanying trifle from
" Your ob't serv't,
" E. K. KANE.

"Jan. 12th, 1853.

" MRS. FOX."

The few notes quoted above will serve to show the
early relations of the parties.

One day, after the company had retired, Dr. Kane,
who had now established himself on the footing of a
friend, lingered in the parlor, and drawing Miss Fox
aside, conversed with her in a low tone, while her

mother was occupied in some other part of the rooms. He again spoke of the melancholy way in which she was living—pursuing a calling which the world thought ambiguous at least, and deplored the fact that deceit was generally attributed to those who engaged in such matters. He reminded her that she was fitted by nature for better things: for the highest destiny of woman. He asked earnestly if she would be willing to quit for ever her present life, and devote herself to acquiring an education, with such habits as would efface the memory of the past, and fit her for an entirely different sphere. "And when you are thus changed, Maggie," he said, "I shall be proud to ·make you my wife. Can you resolve to leave all that surrounds you—with that end in view; to begin your life over again; to forget the past, and think only how you may become worthy of one whose existence shall be devoted to you?"

The young girl answered that she could.

But Dr. Kane saw that the regard he had been able to inspire was not as deep as his own love; how could it be, in one less than half his own age! He wished to see her less of the child, and more of the woman.

"Are you able to feel, Maggie," he said, "how sacred, how binding, is a promise of this kind? It is a plighting of your troth: a solemn surrender of yourself—heart, soul, and life—to another. Do you feel that it is so? Think long and deeply upon it,

and make no promise rashly ; for once made, it must
be inviolable for life. You must not engage yourself to be my wife unless you can give me all your
love—your whole heart; unless you can sacrifice for
me all other anticipations and prospects."

Much more he said on the subject, and gave a history of his own past life ; a brief and barren history,
so far as matters of the heart were concerned. He
told her that his father had wished to see him united
to a lady who possessed wealth, but had no attractions
to fetter his love; and that he had heretofore been
willing to give up his own inclinations in compliance
with the wish of one to whom he owed obedience.
But now the case was entirely altered. He loved for
the first time in his life; he loved deeply, ardently,
and so long as the object of his love continued worthy
of it, his affection would be unchanged. He could
not now bestow his hand where his heart could not
be given. He would immediately release himself from
any supposed obligation on his part to do so. He
would inform his father that his union with Miss ——
was an utter impossibility. Thus he was free to
pledge himself to the bright and blooming and guileless young creature whose sweet dark eyes had capti-
vated him, and who alone should be his in the most
sacred of all ties, when she had set herself free from
trammels of another kind. Margaret listened to all
this, and accepted the vows of the lover to whom she
looked up with admiration and respect, and with

2*

growing regard. It is manifest, however, that she felt as yet none of the impassioned fervor that marked his attachment to her. She was still a child in heart.

Immediately after this memorable interview the tea-bell rang, and the young lady, fluttering with her new happiness, was summoned to take her usual place next her mother. It may well be supposed that she did not much justice to the viands on this occasion; but she found opportunity to whisper to her mother—"I have great news to tell you." The secret was communicated in their own room.

Mrs. Fox of course could not be insensible to the advantages, to her daughter at least, of the alliance proffered; but she knew Dr. Kane could not marry till his return from the Arctic seas; that he was even then making preparations for the expedition, and that it must be uncertain whether he ever would return. She did not wish to part with her daughter, in view of these contingencies, for the present, and was not quite willing to place her immediately at school, as Dr. Kane wished. He had many long and earnest conversations with her, before he could bring her to think of a separation.

Some time after Dr. Kane's declaration of his attachment, one of the visitors to the "spirits" said to Miss Fox, "Do you know that gentleman who is so constant an attendant on your levees? It is the great Dr. Kane."

Margaret was familiar with his name, of course,

by this time; but not having the least knowledge of his past life or his achievements, she was utterly ignorant of his "greatness." This may serve to prove that worldly ambition had no share in the favor with which she regarded his suit. She knew that he was not wealthy; in that respect, and in the distinction derived from fashionable accomplishments and surroundings, he was inferior to many gentlemen whom she saw every day. It was his frankness and sincerity, and his brotherly tenderness for her interests, that first attracted her regard. She knew him to be in the right in his views of the life she was then submitting to, and secretly longed for deliverance, that she might enter the gates of that new existence he had pointed out as alone worthy of her powers.

Dr. Kane often invited her to take drives with him, always in the company of some older lady, for he dreaded the tongue of rumor or scandal, and was as anxious to protect her fair name as if she had been his own sister. Mrs. Patterson frequently accompanied them on these excursions. The drives around Philadelphia are very beautiful, and the young lady greatly enjoyed seeing so many new objects of interest. She had a very charming way of expressing her delight in novel and striking scenes; it was so ingenuous, so sweet, unstudied and child-like; so sparkling and irrepressible, yet so marked by a modesty that was almost timidity. It was the buoyant glee of a child, held in check but not dashed by the

fear of breaking bounds, and possibly giving offence.
In her most joyous moments her clear eyes at once
songht sympathy, and seemed to ask if the joy might
be indulged.　Perhaps the continual necessity of
practising self-control, which her professional life
imposed on her, was the cause of this peculiarity of
manner.　Her nature was impulsive, often impetuous,
though so in all gentleness and sweetness; her emo-
tions had ever been those of happiness only; still, she
had learned self-command from being frequently in
the presence of persons uncongenial to her, and the
blending of this habit of reticence with a natural
gaiety which almost defied restraint, made her, as Dr.
Kane expresses it in one of his letters, "a curious
study."　He appears to have endeavored to awaken
in her a love for the beauty of natural scenery, as well
as the treasures of literature.　Meanwhile her duties
at "the spiritual rooms" continued to occupy much of
her time.

On one occasion the lovers went with a party to
Laurel Hill Cemetery.　Miss Fox slipped at the
entrance, and Dr. Kane expressed his regret at such
an accident, saying he was slightly superstitious, and
"would not for the world it had happened."　Leading
her to the family vault of the Kanes, which was then
unfinished, he knocked on the iron door and repeated
the lines from Longfellow's "Psalm of Life:"

> " Art is long, and time is fleeting ;
> And our hearts, though stout and brave,
> Still, like muffled drums, are beating
> Funeral marches to the grave."

Adding, " Here, Margaret, will be *your* last resting-
place !" He then spoke with deep feeling of "Willie,"
his deceased brother, who had suffered much in the
delirium of his last illness ; and added, "Maggie, you
are a godsend to me," as another worthy object of
affection to fill the place of the lost one. They walked
about and looked at the finest monuments in the
cemetery.

Every place worth visiting in or around Philadelphia was shown by Dr. Kane to his betrothed. On
one occasion Dr. and Mrs. Patterson accompanied
them to the family country-seat, "Rensselaer," now
"Fern Rock." When Dr. Kane stepped out of the
carriage Mrs. Patterson whispered, "Miss Fox, Elisha
loves you; I can see that !" After the ladies alighted
Dr. Kane gave his arm to Margaret and led her
around the grounds, stopping at one of the tenants'
houses a few moments to view some curiosity. On
their return, when they would pass a church, Dr.
Kane would sportively propose to go in and preach a
sermon. From this, and his habit of telling his lady-
love of any fault he observed, she playfully called
him "preacher;" a sobriquet he affixed to many of
his letters.

While they were in the carriage Dr. Kane took

hold of Mrs. Patterson's hand, pulled down the glove, and showed Miss Fox a beautiful ring set in black enamel. After taking home that lady and her husband he accompanied Margaret to her hotel, and when they entered her parlor, snatched her ermine and muff, and came stepping daintily in with, "Here comes Johnny with the tea-things!" He remained to spend the evening, and the next day brought three rings for his lady-love's selection of one. Putting aside a splendid diamond set in pearls, she accepted one set in black enamel and wore it as her "engagement ring."

On another drive they passed the Girard House at an hour when the windows were crowded; yet, notwithstanding this, Dr. Kane insisted on stopping in front of it to show its magnificence, while he bowed to his acquaintances as if proud of the beautiful girl by his side. He had good sense enough to separate her from the profession it was still her fate to exercise; and at this time the rappings were not so unpopular as they became afterwards.

Sometimes ladies of his acquaintance came to the sittings, who used very learned language—unintelligible, of course, to the medium. Dr. Kane always amused himself with their affectation, laughing heartily when they were gone. One of them, an old friend of his, once leaned her arm on the back of his chair, when he immediately rose and begged her to be seated. His sensibility to decorum in social intercourse was very acute. He never failed to reprove

Margaret for any piece of carelessness, however tri-
vial, and sometimes gave her a lecture on the manners
of young ladies. He belonged, in fact, to the old
school, and held chivalrously sacred the delicacy of
the fair sex. At one of the sittings an elderly fool
asked if " the spirit of St. Paul was present !" Dr.
Kane instantly took Miss Fox by the arm and led her
out of the room. He did not choose to permit such
irreverence in her presence.

On one of their drives they stopped at a country
inn, and the landlord was introduced by Dr. Kane to
Miss Fox as " the future Mrs. Kane." This was done
also in Washington to the lady of their boarding-house.

Many times the Doctor said to Mrs. and Miss Fox,
that he regretted that his family were in the bustle
of a removal, otherwise the ladies would be invited
to visit at his father's house. He did not appear to
entertain, at that time, any doubt that his friends
would be received with welcome by his relatives.
About this time he wrote the following verses, which
expressed a disquiet daily increasing in his mind.
The " sinful art " referred to is of course the rappings.

" A STORY.

" *Thoughts which ought to be those of Maggie Fox.*

I.

" Once a maiden sat and thought,
    Her hand upon her brow ;
' Tell me, conscience, have I sought
    The life that greets me now ?

Dreary, dreary, dreary,
    Passes life away,—
Dreary, ever dreary,
            The day
Glides on, and weary
    Is my hypocrisy.

II.

"'I wish I was a laughing girl
    Before my father's door,
As merry as the sunbeams
    That danced upon the floor.
As happy as the running stream
    Beneath the moss-grown trees;
And *free* as fly the swallows
    Upon the evening breeze!
            When I was happy, happy,
                Loving the livelong day :
            Happy as the kisses
                That chased my tears away.
            Happy as the hopes
                Which filled my trusting heart,
            Before I knew a sinful wish,
                Or learned a sinful art.'

III.

"Then the maiden sat and wept,
    Her hand upon her brow;
'So long this secret have I kept,
    I can't forswear it now.
It festers in my bosom,
    It cankers in my heart,
Thrice cursed is the slave fast chained
    To a deceitful art!

Dreary, dreary, dreary,
    The garish sunbeams play;
Dreary, ever dreary,
      The day
Glides on, and weary
    Passes my life away.'

IV.

"Then the maiden knelt and prayed:—
  'Father, my anguish see;
Oh, give me but one trusting hope
  Whose heart will shelter me.
One trusting love to share my griefs,
  To snatch me from a life forlorn;
That I may never, never, never
  Thus endlessly from night to morn,
    Say that my life is dreary
      With its hypocrisy;
Dreary, ever dreary,
      The day
Glides on, and weary
    Passes my life away.'

              " PREACHER."

II.

Dr. Kane very often conversed with Mrs. Fox upon his affairs; the duty before him of going to search for Sir John Franklin, the impossibility of his marriage before his return, and his desire that Margaret should complete her education before that event took place; "She must be fitted," he would say, "to occupy a high position in society." He believed her natural abilities sufficient; and he required that she should cultivate them, and acquire all those ladylike accomplishments he had a right to expect that his wife should possess.

Above all things, he desired to have her removed from the peril of daily association with the miscellaneous crowd who attended the spiritual sittings. Even the presence of such persons was dangerous to the delicacy with which nature had so richly endowed Margaret; how long could it hold out against daily conversation with them! On this point he spoke very frequently and with deep feeling.

Books, and music, and flowers—the richest and rarest—were sent and brought by Dr. Kane every day, and sometimes several times a day, to the object of his affection. Once, presenting her with a camellia, he said, "Like you, it must not be breathed upon." His attentions by this time—with all his precautions—could not fail to be noticed in Philadelphia. Miss Fox always took his arm in their walks, which a young lady rarely does unless engaged to the gentleman; and the question,—"'Lish', what pretty girl was that driving—or walking—with you?" became of almost every day occurrence.

The letters received from Lady Franklin by Dr. Kane, were sent for Margaret to read. On one occasion, referred to in the following letter, he sent his brother John to bring them back. He was to wait upon the young lady in the spiritual circle; hence the cautions given.

[Dr. Kane to Miss Fox.]

"Wrap my letters up carefully and give them to this young gentleman. Do write me a long answer, Maggie, giving me all the news.

"I tell you in confidence (do not mention it to him) that he is my brother, and he thinks the package of letters relates to Sir John Franklin and the 'spirits.' If you have company he will not introduce himself. If your mother has come, he will make her acquaintance.

"I was unwilling to call upon you to-night for fear of *talk;* but I told my brother if you had company to show my ring, so as to avoid mentioning names. Do not let him suppose that you have anything more than mere spirit business with me. I say this on your own account.

"You have a fine chance of making my brother tell you all about L——, that interesting lady who is a candidate for matrimony.

"Dear Maggie, I feared you would be lonely; so I sent down my favorite brother to you, in all this snow and rain. Nothing but my real love for you keeps me from coming."

———

They often carried on a little private correspondence when Mrs. Fox was present. Slips like these would be handed to Margaret as "questions," by the Doctor.

"But I fear that you will not write to me letters of *love.*"

"I will return if possible; if not, good-bye. When this party leave, raise both window-curtains."

"Write to me this evening, to Delmonico's, New York; telling me your movements."

"Good-bye."

———

The peculiar signature of the following letter is worthy of attention, as intended to show the writer's independence of "Mrs. Grundy."

"Thank you, dear Maggie, for your kind letter. I have rode in this cold wind nearly eighteen miles; but this afternoon shall see me in your company,

"What say you to to-morrow for our holiday? Ask your mother. Do not be afraid of 'thinking too much' of me. For even if the drear old Polar winter should make me a perpetual exile, the memory of a dead affection would be better than a recollected coolness.

"If you think me afraid of letters, here is my contradiction.

E. K. KANE!

U. S. Navy!!

No. 36 Girard St.!!!

Philadelphia!!!!

Here is the reply of Miss Fox:

"I am delighted, my dear friend, to know that I will have the pleasure of your company this evening.

"But I fear you will be too much fatigued to ride, —will you not?

"Now, Doctor—be candid!—am I not correct when I say you are an enigma past finding out?

"You know I am.   Many thanks for the music.

"Yours very truly,

"MAGGIE.

"SUNDAY MORNING, January, 1853."

The following missive harps again on the theme that so often caused complaint:

[Dr. Kane to Miss Fox.]

"I have received your excellent letter, dear Maggie, and I need hardly say am gratified to find that you write so ably.   You have more *brain* than I gave you credit for.

"My parlor is full of gentlemen, and I cannot get away from New York to-day.   I will, however, go to-night to New Brunswick, and hire a coach on to Trenton, so as to reach you by one o'clock of Sunday.   This great effort will show you how much I regard your wishes.   There is nothing that you can ask, that, if in my power, I would not give.

"Look at the Herald of this morning.   There is an account of a suicide which causes some excitement.   Your sister's name is mentioned in the inquest of the coroner.   Oh, how much I wish that you would quit this life of dreary sameness and suspected deceit.   We live in this world only for the opinions of the good and noble.   How crushing it must be to occupy with them a position of ambiguous respect!

"I will not deliver the kiss.   Such follies I confine to those for whom I have something more than my lips.   I don't kiss everybody, Miss Maggie!

"I must stop.

"Good-bye!

"SATURDAY, 1 P.M."

Here is a missive indicating some faltering of purpose, but it hardly amounted to anything.

[Dr. Kane to Miss Fox.]

"I cannot get away from New York, nor see you on Saturday.   I wrote by mail to tell you of this unlooked for detention; but fearing that the letter will not reach you, I send another by a private messenger.

"As soon as my time is free, I will hire a carriage to New Brunswick, and perhaps be able to reach Philadelphia in time for a Sunday afternoon's ride. Maggie, do you think many friends would take all this trouble for *you?*   Never doubt me any more.

"Your letter surprised me.   I had no idea you

wrote or thought so well and ably. Indeed, you
were born for better things than the annoyances of
your present career.

"You say 'that you do not understand me'—'I
am a riddle'—'an enigma,' and all that nonsense.
Dear Maggie, you understand me very well. You
know that I am a poor, weak, easily deceived man,
and you think that you are an astute, hardly seen-
through woman, managing me as you please. Now
tell me the truth—don't you?

"If you do, you are half right and half wrong. I
am a man rather of facts and stern purposes, than of
woman thoughts and dreamy indolence. My life is
only commencing as far as regards the weary road
ahead of me, and, if Providence prolongs it, I will
leave after me a name and a success.

"But with all this, I am a weak man and a fool;
weak, that I should be caught in the midst of my
grave purposes by the gilded dust of a butterfly's
wing; and a fool because, while thus caught, I smear
my fingers with the perishable color.

"Maggie, dear, you have many traits which lift
you above your calling. You are refined and loveable; and, with a different education, would have
been innocent and artress; but you are not worthy of
a permanent regard from me. You could never lift
yourself up to my thoughts and my objects; *I* could
never bring myself *down* to yours. This is speaking
very plainly to my dear confiding little friend Maggie

Fox, who sometimes thinks she loves me more than a friend. But Maggie, darling, don't care for me any more. I love you too well to wish it, and you know now that I really am *sold* to different destinies; for just as you have your wearisome round of daily money-making, I have my own sad vanities to pursue. I am as devoted to my calling as you, poor child, can be to yours. Remember then, as a sort of dream, that Doctor Kane of the Arctic Seas loved Maggie Fox of the Spirit Rappings."

[Dr. Kane to Miss Fox.]

" I will see you, if time or money can achieve it, by Sunday at one or two o'clock; you will ride with me.

" Answer to Girard street, as I will go there first if I get back, dear Maggie, and we will talk the thing over.

" The Herald will tell you of this horrid self-murder. How disgusting that the name of the sister of my friend should appear thus in newspaper print!

" I send you the 'Haunted Ground.' It haunts me to see you perched over a twopenny song with ' Margaretta ' in great big print underneath you.

" Maggie, will you promise me not to say anything of this letter to your mother until you see me? Not one word; I have reasons for it. But write at once,

3

that is, by ten or before of Sunday morning, saying if I can see you by two o'clock, and if you think you can ride. If you say so I will bring Mrs. —— to prevent any doubts with your excellent mother. I always want to treat you both with respect."

———

Before the engagement, when Dr. Kane called to pay his respects on New Year's day, Miss Fox asked him to walk into the back room, a splendid apartment furnished with blue damask, to see a cake that had been sent to them. The room had a bed in it. Dr. Kane drew back, and gave the young lady a lecture on the impropriety of inviting a gentleman to pass through a sleeping apartment. So scrupulous was he in matters of etiquette, and so anxious to impress on the young girl the importance of fastidious attention to such things.

III.

In January Mrs. Fox left Philadelphia and went with her daughters to New York, where they took up their residence in Twenty-Sixth street. The younger sister was obliged occasionally to sit in the spiritual circles, though under the direction and charge of another and older person, who was also a medium for the "manifestations." Dr. Kane soon followed them from Philadelphia.

The following letter was sent during the Doctor's absence, while Miss Fox was in New York.

[Dr. Kane to Miss Fox.]

SUNDAY NIGHT.

"MAGGIE DARLING:—Why do you not write to me? Have you forgotten your friend? Or does your new life drive from you the recollection of old times?

"I go to Baltimore on Tuesday, and then to Washington to see the President. Oh, dear Maggie, when I think of you in your humble calling, and of myself with my toiling vanities and cares, I only feel that I am about to leave you; and feeling this, how very, very, very much I love you.

"I am a fool for this, yet I know that you have some good reason for not writing. Send me a lock of your hair; for unless it comes I will not come on to see you.

"Kiss Katy for me, and tell her I am *your* friend, and therefore her own. If ever trouble presses his cold hand—colder, Maggie, than the spirits, come to your one friend, for he alone has no coldness. Remember his warm hands, his glowing kisses, and his steadfast, trusting heart; and then you cannot forget him.

"Write to me how I can see you if I come to New York. How can I meet you, dear Maggie, away from suspicion, away from Mrs. —— ? Do you ever walk out alone?

"God bless you!"

The "suspicion" he feared was that of spiritualist friends, who fancied they had an exclusive right to Maggie's time and attention. Fear, too, of the censure of his friends, caused a wish for concealment evident in many of his letters.

————

[Dr. Kane to Mrs. Fox.]

"WASHINGTON, January 27th, 1853

"MY DEAR MADAM:—I forward, by express, a copy of 'Undine' for my friend Miss Maggie.

"It was my intention to have been in New York by Saturday; but a compulsory engagement in

Washington detains me. I hope, however, to visit your city in the early part of next week, and I will of course pay my respects as soon as my time permits.

> "In haste, your ob't servant,
> "E. K. KANE."

———

The following is marked "*Letter No. 2*" in the Doctor's handwriting. Many letters preceded it, however. The cautious tone of the latter part arose from fears of giving offence to Margaret's hostess, who was jealous of aught that drew her attention from her friends.

[Dr. Kane to Miss Fox.]

"DEAR MAGGIE:—I have just received your letter, for which I thank you. But upon comparing it with my own, I confess that all the warmth and affection seem to be on my side. You write to me entirely as to a friend—a kind, non-committal letter. I write as to a lover, overflowing with the feeling of the moment. Do you know, Maggie, that I am now almost ashamed to send the letter which accompanies this?

"Your life must be dreary, dear darling; dreary with its sameness; dreary with the mysterious workings of the spirit world. I held up my hand the other night, just about twilight, in the dusk of the evening. You know what I felt and saw.

"I miss you when I look over my crowded table, with its books and papers. I miss you when I mount my horse for one of my wild rides. I miss you when listening to the empty nonsense of my fashionable friends, who think themselves so much better than yourself. What is it that I miss in Maggie Fox, that I cannot find in them? I'll tell you. It is not beauty, for they are as beautiful as you. It is not kind words or demonstrations, for they go further than you. But it is in that strange mixture of child and woman, of simplicity and cunning, of passionate impulse and extreme self-control, that has made you a curious study. Maggie, you are *very* pretty, very childlike, very deceitful, but to me as *readable* as my grandmother's Bible.

" Write me word by post or by my friend, whether you are happy, and if I, your friend, can do nothing for you. Walk out every day alone or with Kate, and then if I should come to New York, we can easily see each other without exciting the suspicions of ——you know who.

"So much do I care for you, that I am at any sacrifice about to visit New York, and that, too, before the *millennium*. But, dear darling, think how I am overwhelmed with responsible duties !

"The highest compliment I can pay you is to tell

you what I have before me, that you may judge of
what an effort it is to see you. On Tuesday, I lecture
before three thousand persons in Baltimore; on
Wednesday, meet the great men of Washington; on
Thursday, explain the Expedition to the scientific
bodies; on Friday come home, and on Saturday—go
to my little Maggie.

"Do have a letter to meet me in Philadelphia, at
Girard street, written and sent off on Wednesday
from New York: stating how your hours are filled
up. 2. The names and character and appearance of
the servants. 3. Whether you can see me at any
time alone. Had I better call with Mr. —— on
Saturday evening? I think not, for you will be full
of company. Write me word.

"Maggie, do you know Satler's Cosmoramas in
Broadway near Twelfth street, on the right hand side
going down? If you and Kate will walk past it at
exactly four o'clock on Saturday afternoon, I will be
there. The cosmoramas are a sort of picture gallery,
visited by the first and best ladies. If you and Kate
do not like to walk past, go up into the picture-room,
and amuse yourselves looking at the paintings until
you see me. I will be there at four precisely, and
wait till half-past four. You have to pay twenty-five
cents admission, so don't forget your purse. I will
bring a supply of *pocket-handkerchiefs*.

"Write me word if you can do this, so that I may
get the letter on Friday; and if anything goes wrong,

a letter directed to Delmonico's Hotel will reach me. Good-bye."

Miss Margaret had a fashion, it seems, of always losing her handkerchiefs. Her reply to the foregoing was as follows:

[Miss Fox to Dr. Kane.]

"You will pardon me, my dear friend, for not meeting you. Strange, that I should have made such a promise—so imprudent! My mind at that time must have been so much upon * * that I overlooked things of far greater importance to me. How must it look in your eyes (and surely I care as much for you as any one)!

"The idea seems to me so unbecoming. I do not care half as much for strangers, or the opinion of others, as I do for myself. But if you will call here I will go; and should be most happy to do so, as I have no other engagement during the day. Yours evermore.

"I send this by my servant, but very much fear she will not find you.

"Write on a card or piece of paper; then ring the bell and tell the servant to take it to me. I will read it to Mrs. ——, and she will think well of it.

"MAGGIE."

Being in New York, just on the eve of another
journey, Dr. Kane sent the following :—

[Dr. Kane to Miss Fox.]

"DEAREST MAGGIE :—Do say when I can see you.
I leave for Boston to-morrow at three P.M. to be gone
for a week. Do write to Revere House. You never
write to me, Maggie. At what hour may I call
to-morrow ?"

———

The following letters were written before Miss Fox
left New York for Washington.

[Dr. Kane to Miss Fox.]

"DEAR, DEAR MAGGIE :—Have you ceased to care
for me ? *me* whose devotion you now can see, and of
whose true, steadfast love every fibre of your heart
assures you !

"I called on you this morning on my way to
Boston. Kate and your mother said you were out;
but ah, Maggie, you forget my *hand*. Do you want
me to cease my attentions? Say so, dear Maggie,
and even if it kills me I will not annoy you; God
knows I love you too much to give you pain or
trouble.

"Maggie, do see me. Cannot you and Kate leave

3*

the house at ten to-morrow morning, turn to the right until you come to the first cross street, when upon turning again to the right you will see me. Do, dear Maggie, do! You leave for Washington soon; so what can it matter even if it costs you a few words with * * * ?

"Tell Kate how much I thank her. She is a dear good girl; show her this letter."

[Dr. Kane to Miss Fox.]

"DEAR TUTIE:—I will send a carriage at eleven o'clock precisely for you (*dear* Maggie) to go to the dressmaker's, where I will meet you.

"Give my compliments to your mother, and tell her that, with her permission, I should like you and your sister to devote the rest of the day to a fine ride with your friend.

"I have taken the liberty of buying you a tra-velling bonnet, which I will send to you this morning.

"Your friend,

"E. K. KANE."

IV.

Mrs. Fox and her two youngest daughters, Margaret and Katharine, were at Washington in the latter part of the winter on a professional visit. Governor Tallmadge (the Governor of Wisconsin) procured lodgings for them at Mrs. Sullivan's house, where many officers were accustomed to stay.

Their first news from the absent friend was in the telegraphic despatch, copied here to illustrate his devotion.

"Dated BOSTON, Feb. 12th, 1853.
"Rec'd Washington.
"To MISS FOX, at Mrs. Sullivan's,
"F. street, 3 doors west 13th.

"Has your bonnet arrived? Telegraph how you are, and how you all like Washington.

"E. K. KANE."

It was speedily followed by a letter.

On the 13th February Mayor Seaver gave a dinner to a party of select friends at the Revere House, Boston. Among the guests were Dr. Kane and Chief Justice Shaw.

Dr. Kane sent the bill of fare to his friend with this brief note.

"Here is a specimen of a good dinner to feast the

eyes of my friend Miss Kate. The service was of gold and glass."

——————

With the following letter from Boston Dr. Kane sent an extract from a Boston paper.

[Dr. Kane to Miss Fox.]

"DEAR MAGGIE-FRIEND:—Your telegraph has reached me, saying that you have written, and asking an immediate answer. It will reach me to-morrow. How I long to know what that letter says, to see whether it bears marks of love and affection. I will answer it at once.

"How I long, dear friend, to be with you! My illness has left me thin, and weak, and wretched; but there is no rest; I must work for my great enterprise.

"Try, dear Maggie, to do your duty in this world. Be true to your loves; be true to yourself; and when that rarest of God's gifts, a loving heart, comes to you again, ' grapple it with hooks of steel.'

"God bless you, Maggie.

"P. S.—How disgusting is this life, to be discussed by the papers! I need not be so proud, Maggie, for I am no better than the 'rappers.'

"Read this:

"Revere ——, Feb. 17, 1853.

"Dr. Kane's Lecture.—A highly intelligent audience assembled at the Lecture Room of the new Music Hall, last evening, to hear Dr. Kane. They listened with profound attention and with tokens of delight to one of the most interesting lectures we have heard for a long time. Dr. Kane's name is familiar to the public in connexion with the 'Grinnell Expedition' to the Polar regions, and, lately, connected with the new expedition which he is to command.

"He is a small man, slightly made, full of energy, intelligence, and enthusiasm, and with an organization which makes one think of Damascus steel. His manner is modest and winning, and his agreeable voice, choice language, and gentlemanly deportment, would give interest to the most commonplace topic; while his theme, on which no man is better prepared to speak, would command the attention of an audience without the very pleasant magnetism of his manner.

"He spoke of the fatality which has attended explorers in Arctic regions; of the *cui bono* of such researches; and gave an account of various events of the Grinnell Expedition, speaking particularly of the long drift of the Advance and the Rescue in the ice.

"Dr. Kane will deliver his next lecture on Thursday evening. In this lecture, we believe, he will discuss the probable fate of Sir John Franklin. He cannot fail of a crowded house."

"DEAREST MAGGIE:—After my hard day's work is over, I come home to my hotel rooms and think of you. Your friend is hardly worked, for science knows no rest to its votaries, and my toil cannot have an interruption. Looking ahead, I see no prospect of meeting you in Washington for at least a fortnight. Oh, Maggie! do you feel as sorry for this compulsory absence as I do?

"My lectures here have been most successful, drawing around me all the wealth and beauty of this great city; but I speak for humanity, and not for money. When I think of you, dear darling, wasting your time and youth and conscience for a few paltry dollars, and think of the crowds who come nightly to hear of the wild stories of the frozen north, I sometimes feel that we are not so far removed after all. My brain and your body are each the sources of attraction, and I confess that there is not so much difference.

* * * * *

" For me, a grave man of science and hard labor, to write thus to you, would be thought very strange by the meddling world; but, dear darling Maggie, where I love, *I* confide; and where I confide, I never think of caution. Do be careful of me and my reputation, for I would die rather than injure yours.

" The laces will come to you by express;—one, an

under-handkerchief of *Honiton*, with sleeves to match; the other of French work, for morning wear. Do be careful and dress well about your neck and arms, for I want my Maggie to appear as a lady wherever she is.

"One of the very first things that drew me towards you, was your ladylike manner and deportment. A little affectation about it, but still very gentle and quiet, and modest, and retiring, as a lady's should be. Keep up this, dear Maggie, and never indulge in any *spirit jokes* with the Washington people.

"In fact, I would never allow myself to be jocular with 'the spirits,' unless before 'cousin Leib' and myself. People will be suspicious if you do. Keep a grave face, and decline replying to jesting questions.

"You have not written, at least had not up to Monday night. I love you too well to complain. I do all the writing, all the talking, and I fear, all the loving. Never yet have you said upon paper,— 'Cousin Peter, I love you.' It is always 'dear friend.' Very well;—'dear friend.' Better that than nothing. Take care!!

"When I come on, Maggie, we will have nice times, riding every day, and living like old times in Philadelphia.

"Kiss Katy for me; tell her she owes me a letter. She is worth two of you.

"Bye bye.

"PREACHER."

"How does Washington come on? Many beaux? Many believers? Many friends? Answer these questions, you wicked little Maggie!

"Do you want some advice? It's a very cheap article. Never venture out in Washington except in the very best company. If you can get a *real* gentleman, grab him; but have nothing to do with the vulgar members of Congress. If you have not had an opportunity of seeing the sights, wait till your friend comes; he has ballast enough to steady you, and is not ashamed to escort you anywhere.

"Wear your undersleeves and spencer *always* when you have company. I sent a rich ladylike set for morning wear, and another of *Honiton lace* for evening occasions. Do wear them, Maggie, and tell Kate that as soon as I get back to Philadelphia, I will send her a *real appliquée*. My sister got one, and they are a very rich character of lace.

"I am anxious that you two girls should be well dressed; in fact, dear Maggie, you can hardly realize how much I care for you, and how often I think of you.

Now that I know you do not love me, I feel as if I would like to show you how good, and true, and disinterested a friend you have lost. No, dear Maggie, lost is not the word; you have only lost a lover. I will always be your friend.

"I am very sick, and it was only last night that I made the discovery of not possessing your love. I will never hold up my hand again—for I would rather have remained in ignorance; but the thing is done, and can't be helped. I shall not come to Washington now, for I am ashamed to say that I care so much for you that it would increase my unhappiness. Good-bye, then, my still dear Maggie, and if there be any-thing in my power to give you, always remember that you have at least one person who, knowing all, cares for you unselfishly and truly for yourself alone. I shall always be your friend, and perhaps you are glad to get rid of me in the other relation!

"God bless you."

————

[Dr. Kane to Miss Fox.]

"MAGGIE—I am sick—sick at the hotel—sick with hard work, and with nobody to nurse or care for me. You saw how wretchedly I looked when in New York; I am far worse now, and without any chance of resting. Is it any wonder, then, that I long to be with you, to have again the lazy days, and sit by your side talking nonsense!

"Is it any wonder that I long to look—only to look—at that dear little deceitful mouth of yours; to feel your hair tumbling over my cheeks, as I write the spirit messages from another world—*our* world, Maggie—the world of love!

"It is Sunday, and I am just back from a large dinner party. To-morrow, if I am well enough, I lecture, and I fear will have to stay throughout the week in this miserable rainy town of Boston.

"Rain—rain—rain! When it rains the lovers in heaven are quarrelling. I expect they quarrel for ever in the Boston paradise. Did ever Christian man see such an incessant leaking from the skies?

"Maggie, if I had my way with you, I would send you to school and learn you to live your life over again. You should forget the r—pp—gs (I never mention the name now), and come out like gold purified from the furnace; a pure simple-hearted *trusting* girl. Once that, Maggie, and you would love me; not the sort of *half-affected* milk and water love which you now profess, but a genuine, confiding affection. Your eyes would be opened and you would see me as I am. Seeing me *as I am*, you would *have* to love me.

"Now to you I am nothing but a cute, cunning dissembler; a sort of smart gentleman hypocrite, never really sincere, and merely amusing himself with a pretty face. This is because you view me with the suspicious, distrusting eyes which your short intercourse with the world—*your world*—has forced upon you. You flatter yourself that this is *penetration*, and that you can read motives and character.

"Poor girl! Take care that you do not lose the only friend you ever had in your life; for until you look deeper you will never *love* me; and unless you love me I will soon cease to love you.

"Do, dear Maggie, learn that my 'acuteness' is only the result of the life which in my station I am forced to lead. That it covers a warm manly heart, that I can never say to you an untrue word. That in trouble I would be your refuge, in joy your sympathizer; that I do this unselfishly, looking only to your happiness, and never thinking of any thing which could lessen you in your eyes or me in my own.

"Learn to believe all this, and think what you will fling away if you do not love me. Believe me, Maggie, I can tell when it is present, and you know that you do not love me. I rather like you for this, because if you were entirely artful and selfish you would pretend to love me for the sake of your own interests. I am glad that you don't pretend, but until you look upon me with trust and brotherly confidence you can never love me. You will have to do this soon, Maggie; for some morning you will wake up and find that your friend is for ever lost to you. I do these things in a very queer way. Some day or other I will say to myself, 'Am I not injuring my dignity by thus throwing away upon a person in a walk of life different from my own, feelings which she can never understand and of which she is not worthy!' This question I will answer for myself, and if the answer be against you, Maggie, you will see me no more.

"Excuse this cruel way of writing; but it is better that you should understand me. If I did not so love that dark-eyed little Maggie of mine, I would not write to her thus. That Maggie Fox must see me in my true character or she will never see me. Do then, dear, dear, dear darling, give me your whole heart and soul! You may have mine in return; and once convinced that you are really mine in love, there will be no end to my confidence and affection! I am very sick, Maggie, but I hope not cross. Don't be hurt at what I say, but write to me by every mail. I cannot leave Boston for a week or more.

"God bless you!"

During a serious illness Dr. Kane sent several telegraphic despatches.

[Miss Fox to Dr. Kane.]

"My dear Dr. Kane:—I received both the despatches, and this afternoon received your letter; many thanks. I am grieved to hear that you are ill. You say that you will telegraph every day. Do not forget to do so, for I am uneasy about you. This afternoon I went out to do some shopping, and lost my way. I grew so frightened that I was obliged to

ask a lady to show me the way home. When I
entered the room I cried aloud; and looking up I
saw General Hamilton, who asked me what was the
matter. I told him I had lost my way, and that I did
not like Washington at all. He laughed heartily,
and insisted upon it that no young lady could ever
lose her way in Washington unless she had some
'*affaire du cœur.*' I did not deny the charge. Doctor,
there is a rumor—so the General tells me—that you
and I are to be married before you go to the Arctic.
Last evening I saw a large company of officers. I
believe they took me for the 'spirit,' for they looked
at me so incessantly that I nearly fainted; and I
heard one gentleman ask his friend sitting next to him
'if Miss Fox did not attend the ball.' His friend did
not seem to know; when he very coolly asked me,
'if I was not at the ball given by Mrs. B——,' I told
him I was not there. He said if it was not myself it
must *certainly* have been my apparition. He was a
Frenchman.

" Ever most truly yours,

" MAGGIE."

V.

The following letters are preserved, among others, written about this time. This to Miss Katharine Fox is evidently designed to excite the jealousy of her sister, if that could be done.

[Dr. Kane to Miss Kate Fox.]

"DEAR MISS INCOMPREHENSIBLE KATE :—I have never yet written you a long letter; but your sister has doubtless told you that I have formally resigned every thing but her friendship; so that henceforward you are both of you alike in my eyes; and I do not see why you should not take half of my correspondence. As a friend, I think you will like me quite as well as in the other relation; and I am sorry to say that your sister will like me better. Oh, Katy, could you not keep a little fire in the ashes of my memory? Why did you let that fickle, wicked little Maggie forget me? I'm glad, however, that I found it out in time; for the discovery goes hard enough with me as it is.

"Well, now for talk. Boston is a funny place, and 'the spirits' have friends here. You would be surprised if I told you what I have heard. There is one gentleman here, high in position and intellect, who keeps a medium in his house. This is no great hardship, for she is very pretty; but do you know that he only visits her twice a day, with a list of questions as long as my arm? He governs every action of life by the answers, and is worse than a dozen Dr. Notts or Mr. Longface Kennedys.

" There is a very refined lady here who took me to see the thing. I kept one of my grave faces, and was appropriately patronized. Chairs danced about the room, and clothes were twitched to an extent far ahead of Mrs. ——. By the bye, I will teach you this last mystery, for I believe that you do not know it. Believing as implicitly as I do in the spirits, of course I am excusable for finding out the twitching.

" There are some things that I have seen which I think would pain you. Maggie would only laugh at them; but with me it gave cause for sadness. I saw a young man, with a fine forehead and expressive face, but a countenance deeply tinged with melancholy, seize the hand of this *medium*, whose name— as I never tell other persons' secrets—I cannot tell you. He seized her hand, and begged her to answer a question which I could not hear. Instantly she rapped, and his face assumed a positive agony; the rapping continued, his pain increased; I leaned forward, feeling an utter detestation for the woman who could inflict such torment; but it was too late. A single rap came, and he fell senseless in a fit. This I saw with my own eyes.

"Now, Katy, although you and Maggie never go
so far as this, yet circumstances must occur where you
have to lacerate the feelings of other people. I know
that you have a tender heart; but practice in anything hardens us. You do things now which you
would never have dreamed of doing years ago; and
there will come a time when you will be worse
than ——; a hardened woman, gathering around you
victims of a delusion. Think of that, Katy!

"The older you grow the more difficult it will be
to liberate yourself from this thing. And can you
look forward to a life unblessed by the affections,
unsoothed by the consciousness of doing right! For
you, no innocence with the blessings of a kindly home
is now in store. When your mother leaves this scene
can you and my still dear Maggie be content to live
that life of constant deceit? Do, dear Katy, think of
all this!

"A few weeks ago I would have put forth my arm
to save you; I would have been to you and your
sister that which, from a gentleman in my position,
you will never have again; but, dear Katy, this has
passed. I am not now willing to make the sacrifice
which *that* would have demanded; for it would be
unaccompanied by a corresponding confidence. I do
not blame poor Maggie, for I am still her best friend;
but she esteemed me too lightly for me ever to be
anything more. I cannot now, dear child, take you
with me.

"But for all that I am still the best friend that you and Maggie have, for I am disinterested; and although your education has taught you suspicion and distrust, you know that I am a man in whom you may confide. Now cannot I help you and Maggie? Is there nothing that I can do to make you more worthy of this world *and the next?* Do, Kate, try and think over it, and call upon your friend if he can help you.

"I have taken the liberty of getting you, also, a Honiton set. I will be in Washington soon, and although I cannot perhaps see you, will send it to your establishment. Do not think it strange if I should not call, for I am a person of strong will; and after having made up my mind do not like to subject myself to temptation. Besides, you know, Katy, that I am right, and that Maggie deserves this."

[Dr. Kane to Miss Fox.]

"DEAR MAGGIE:—I know that you will be tempted to open Kate's letter, so I send it through you in order that I may trust in your honor.

"If you want to see it show Kate this note, and tell her that I wish you to see the contents. I say nothing except that *we* are *only friends* and giving *her* a friend's advice."

4

Miss Maggie's reply to this letter complaining of her want of affection, shows what a simple child she was.

"MY DEAR FRIEND:—Your letter was received this morning; strange, strange letter.

"Then I have lost, forever lost, the friend I loved so dearly! Often, while reading your letter to Kate, an involuntary tear started to my eyelid. I could not check it. Oh! how I have longed to be with you, but can hardly expect to again.

"I will look back with pleasure on those hallowed hours I have passed with you.

"Should we never again meet in this world we will in another. Then you will *know* I have loved you, and love you still.

"Farewell.

"Oh, how sorry I am to hear you are ill! I wish I could be with you!

"As ever, yours,
"MAGGIE."

———

Miss Kate was again favored.

"DEAR MISS KATE:—I hope that you are well and

happy, and that you have not forgotten your promises to your friend.

"Take my advice and never talk of the spirits either to friends or strangers; you know that with all my intimacy with Maggie, after a whole month's trial, I could make nothing out of them. Therefore they are a *great mystery*.

"So never speak of them lightly even to your best friends.

"If ever I can be of use to you call on me, as well on your sister's account as on your own. I would be glad to serve you.

"Good bye."

———

[Dr. Kane to Miss Fox.]

"MAGGIE DARLING :—Go quietly to the solitude of your room before you read this ; for I have never yet written to you, *as myself*, and I am now for the first time about to pay you the compliment of a good, honest letter of simple truth.

"Your last letter—the only one received since my sickness—that in which you speak of the malignant influences of 'rainy days'—has shown me that you possess more mind than I gave you credit for. Try then, dear Maggie, to comprehend what I am about to say ; to see me shining through my words like the gildings of the mists upon which you have discoursed such pretty music.

"Who am I? Answer that question first. Ponder over it, and see what are my prospects as regards worldly wealth, intellectual character, public estimation, and family name. That, dear, dear little Maggie, ask yourself. What are to be my destinies: and talking to you in the pure simplicity of confidence, I will answer that question myself.

First, I am better, *nobler* in moral tone than I have seemed to you. My conscience urges me to a crusade of rescue for our lost men, now wandering in an icy wilderness; and for it and them I am about to sacrifice the thousand dear things of life, home, luxury, and *love*.

"After spending from my private means, that which would to you be a *fortune*, I am about to spend the treasured years of a lifetime, perhaps life itself.

"This, dear Maggie, speaking to you plainly, is your friend. Born in circles of pleasure, and sought wherever he chose to seek, he one day, to pass an idle hour, called upon a something which he had heard of, in half sneering parlance, as the 'spiritual rappings.'

"There he saw a little *Priestess*, cunning in the mysteries of her temple, and *weak* in every thing but the power with which she played her part. A sentiment almost of pity stole over his worldly heart as he saw through the disguise. Don't be angry, dear, dear Maggie! 'Can it be that one so young, so beautiful, so passionate, and yet so kind hearted, can be destined for such a life?' These were his thoughts.

"Thereupon he went to work and did all that true kindness could do to get her confidence. Never, in the many hours that followed, did he leave a wish of hers ungratified, or say or think an unkindly word. His sad destinies in behalf of humanity forbid him to dwell in the regions of *love*—and then like a fool he went on *loving*.

"Why was this, dear little Maggie? It was because you had, knowing all the circumstances, said and written 'love on!' and therefore, dear darling, I forgot my high calling and let myself *down to love*.

"'And now why all this nonsense?' I think I hear you say. 'Why, I knew all this before.'

"Maggie, I've an object in writing. Read on.

"The fool so far forgot himself as actually to care for you. When absent he dreampt of you and recalled the dear hours of pleasure which he had lost. There was nothing that he would not have done; and in spite of his public duties and the adulation of the world, his thoughts constantly reverted to the out of the way little corner of one Maggie Fox. At the very dinner table of the President he thought of her. Wonderful to relate, he even banished ——. You never comprehended him, Maggie; you held him too cheaply.

"One day he was thinking it all over. He felt her warm kisses on his lips, her long hair sweeping his cheeks. There was nothing at that moment that he would not have done for her. He would raise her above her calling, even to his own level; he would cultivate her mind, give her a competence; her sister should be his care. Maggie, there is nothing that he would not have done. * * * * *. When for the first time came the thought, what am I about to do for this woman? Does she love me enough to make it right that I should sacrifice so much for her? Not the *money*—for she is beyond money in *my* eyes—but the *love;* does she love me as I should be loved?

"Then I thought it all over, dear Maggie, all the little evidences (you know how *cute* I am) of affection. I saw that you loved me, but not enough. Dear child, it was not in your nature. You would give me everything when near me, but forget me when away. So I made up my mind, and in a moment you became *my friend.*

"Don't be hurt or angry, dear, sweet Maggie, for you have by this time learned to know me. Our intercourse will be as a dream, coming back to you in the quiet reveries of life's summer time, when I am buried in the *Polar snows.*

"Strange are the mysteries of the heart; and now that it is too late, you will love me as before you did not. You will never be able to recall any thing about me little, or mean, or selfish; and you will have upon you, like a momentary nightmare, the sad conviction of what you have lost.

"Don't think, Maggie darling, that I am blaming you, or that I am suspicious, or cross, or peevish; I

never said an unkind thing to you in my life. I only
tell you in manly straightforwardness that which your
own heart acknowledges, 'that you had not the depth
of affection to be worthy of me.'

" Change is a principle of our nature ordained by a
law of God, and impressed upon every living thing.
The humble lowliness of the budding plant expands
into the painted glories of the flower, and the oak of
the spring-time is not the oak of winter. We all
change, dear Maggie, and *novelty* is the mother of one
half of our blessings. Do not think that I blame you
for obeying an instinct of your nature.

"Your letter, the only letter up to Tuesday the
16th, makes me write to you thus.

"Now hear my conclusion. Put your little hand
upon your heart, and say—' He places confidence in
me and tells me the actual truth; shall I reward his
candor by deception ?' And then sit down at once,
dear Maggie, and write to me, and I will believe you.
If it be that you really in your deepest centre care for
me, say so; if it be the feeling of a friend only, say
so; and in the one case I will see you again; in the
other, never.

" Direct your letter at once to Delmonico's. I leave
Boston on Saturday.

" Think over this letter ! ! !"

Like Surrey's Geraldine—

> "She had not years to understand
> The grief that he did feel."

VI.

When Dr. Kane and his brother came to Washington, they were unable to get rooms at a hotel, and took them, accordingly, in Mrs. Sullivan's house. Their parlour was on the floor above that occupied by Mrs. Fox. But, though lodging under the same roof, Dr. Kane jealously observed the same formal etiquette with the ladies, as if they had been in their own mansion. He once spoke seriously to the younger ones on the impropriety of calling to gentlemen, or knocking at the doors of their private parlors. Miss Fox had too much intuitive delicacy to make such cautions necessary; indeed, she would have been called prudish by most American young women.

"The Preacher's" homilies, however, did not prevent his own dereliction sometimes. On one occasion, after knocking at Mrs. Fox's parlor door for admission in vain (a private circle was in session), he sent in the following slip:

"Maggie, you are a d——d humbug! I refused a dinner at the French Minister's——the Count de Sartiges——for the pleasure which you now deny me. D——n Waddy!——send your mother, at least."

At another time, impatient of the sittings—while one was going on, he sent in a note, beseeching his "Dearest Pet" to

"Come out for a moment from those coarse people ——to your friend waiting for his little Maggie. Surely you can rest a minute! Come, dearest fluttering bird! Come!"

———

On one occasion, after a large company of gentlemen had left the spiritual rooms, Miss Fox heard the familiar knock of her friend at the door; and being inclined for a little girlish mischief, concealed herself in the wardrobe, which had been placed in the room for the purpose of exhibiting some extraordinary manifestation when the medium was within it. Dr. Kane opened the door, and advancing to the table, took up and read the questions that had been written in the circle. Then he soliloquized aloud. It was such a pity!—It was so repulsive—so abhorrent to refinement—to be exposed to such associations! It was so wounding to his feelings, to have one he held so dear, compelled to mingle in such society! "To think of my Maggie listening to such questions!" The lesson was not lost on the young lady, who heard all in her hiding-place.

At another time the Doctor entered the parlor just

4*

as poor Maggie had accidentally pulled down a cup of cough syrup from the mantelpiece over her head and neck. The lover hurried to her assistance, and carefully washed her hair, face, and neck, delighted to perform any kind office for her, and snatch the opportunity of kissing the disarranged locks and wet forehead.

It could hardly have been a lover's quarrel that called forth such notes as the following; one of a hundred :

"So, Miss Maggie, you have given me up. Well !
"Good-bye."

———

Carriages were very expensive in Washington at that time, yet Dr. Kane procured them for his friends without regard to cost, and Miss Fox was taken to see all the lions of the Federal City. The Doctor tried his voice in the Smithsonian Institution, with a view to a lecture. Once, when driving out, at sight of some cows, the young lady expressed a desire to drink a cup of fresh milk. He insisted on procuring it for her at a house by the road side. Her slightest wish was realized by him, and anticipated whenever it was possible.

———

Miss Fox suffered from influenza in Washington,
while Dr. Kane was absent; a telegraphic despatch,
bearing date March 11th, 1853, sent while he was in
Philadelphia, was in these words:

" Are you better?
"Shall I come to you?

"E. K. KANE."

One dated the day previous was as follows:

"March 10th, 1853.

To MISS MARGARET FOX,
F. Street, 3 doors west of 13th Street, Washington.

When do you leave?   Answer by bearer.
E. K. KANE.
36 Girard Street."

———

These letters followed the despatch;

[Dr. Kane to Miss Fox.]

"PHIL'A, March 10th, '53.

'MISS M. FOX.

"Very, very sorry, dear darling, that you are sick.
Sick in gloomy Washington, with nobody to sympathize with you, except fusty old Tallmadge, and fool-

ish Waddy Numbskull. Do you not miss the kind welcome, the greeting smile, the warm kiss, and the resting breast of 'cousin Peter?' Do, dear Maggie, hurry and leave this wretched life. Come, dear little one, and nestle in my arms. But for the Polar Ices they should be your home.

"Keep up your spirits, and when the vulgar crowd permit you, write to the one person in all the world who 'holds your destinies' in his hands; that trusted and well-beloved friend and *master*, who yet controls not heavily, but leads you to better ways by the cords of *love*."

[Dr. Kane to Miss Fox.]

"DEAR DARLING CHILD:—I am more than sorry at your sickness, and but for your telegraph would have come on to you. If at any moment I can be of use send for me, and regard me as in *every thing* at your service.

"Sign your telegraphs F. Webster.

"I will write again and longer. The mail is clos-ing. Learn to understand me, and remember that you are to live hereafter as one born to a nobler and better life.

"God bless you, little one."

The following despatch was sent as the party was about leaving Washington.

"PHILA., March 14th, 1853.

"To MISS MARGARET FOX,
    "F. st. 3 doors west of 13th st.,
        "Mrs. Sullivan's, Washington.

"Do you leave at five?
"Telegraph your health by bearer.
          "E. K. KANE."

The frequency of these despatches showed the Doctor's warm and impetuous nature. Sometimes three or four in a day would be received by Miss Fox.

The following note awaited Miss Fox at the hotel in Philadelphia.

[Dr. Kane to Miss Fox.]

"Have you arrived? I went to the cars for you with a carriage, but missed you.

"If you come in time go to Madame Barati's, Eighth street below Walnut, for your dress.

"Send word when you wish me to call."

———

The following formal note intervening, was sent *open* by a friend in Philadelphia. It forms a curious contrast to the others, and shows that there had been no avowal among Dr. Kane's friends of his engagement.

"MY DEAR MISS FOX:—I hear with regret that you visit our city during my absence in New York. If you remain in Philadelphia beyond Wednesday, have the kindness to favor me with your address, as I should much like to present you to my father, and reciprocate your courtesy by the hospitalities of our quiet village.

"In haste very faithfully

"Your friend and servant,

"E. K. KANE."

The above was immediately preceded by the following.

"DEAR MAGGIE:—Like a good boy I have been twice to the cars, and twice telegraphed you without an answer. If you should come in to-night, this letter will at least show you that you have one true and devoted friend.

"I have been busy inquiring into schools, and have much news for you.

"Go to-morrow morning to Madame Barati's. Fran-

cis will call at about ten o'clock for your orders. Tell
him at what time to have a carriage for you, and
make use of me and mine as if I were your brother.
Remember that from this time forward you belong to
me. Forget the spirits, and live for better and happier things. Send word by Francis about your movements. And if you don't want to write—for *you*
never write—why take no trouble with cousin *Peter*.

"Love to Kate. Remembrance to Mother Fox."

———

[Dr. Kane to Miss Fox.]

"DEAR MAG :—I have been inquiring after schools
like a good fellow; seeking out *many*, that my little
Maggie may have a choice. I have also written for
a fine Newfoundland dog—a big, brave, steadfast
friend—who will keep love of me alive *in you*.

"Dear Maggie, how happy and proud you will
make me if you study well to improve in all things,
that your life may be a blessing instead of a curse,
and that, in this heartless world of misconstruction, I
can lay the flattering unction to my soul of having
done good to you.

"But I cannot help telling you how much depends
upon *you*, how little upon myself. I will give all that
man and friend can give, but what is that in compa-
rison with what is allotted to you!

"Listen, Maggie; instead of a life of cherished excitement you must settle down into one of quiet, commonplace repose. Instead of the fun, the deli cious merriment of * * * * (we wont trust this to paper), you will have the irksome regulations of a school, the strict formal precepts of a lady abbess, a *schoolmistress.*

"No more Waddys, no more Greeleys, no more wiseacre scientific asses, and pop-eyed committees of investigation! No more sympathizing evenings with your one true friend, nor dinners, and drives to quaint old country inns!!

"Yes, dear darling, you must give up all these, and draw upon your self-denial and energies to sustain you; but then what a return!

"How pleasant, very pleasant, to find yourself developing a new flower—better, a *new woman*—the girl merged in the new career, and a life of usefulness decked with hope and blessings spreading itself before you!

"Do, dear, sweet pet, 'sugar-plum,' *try* hard, struggle hard, fight hard, and be a reward to me. Oh, how happy we will be!

"Amen!

"Oh, how I love you since our ride! You know me just as I am: my good and my bad—for from you I have no concealments. And I know you even to your secret faults, and knowing you, love you. What more can you desire?

"Except God, no one knows you as I do. Make me your guardian angel, dear Maggie, and remember our last *compact*. You know what I mean.

"He is a strange man, this *master* of yours; you love him and honor him; for you see mixed up with his faults much good. Do, dear darling, let me influence you, and guide you to happy paths!

"I promised a horseback ride; I promised to be in New York on Saturday. Well, I never break a promise!

"PREACHER.

"MARCH 17th."

The "compact" was a mutual promise of truth and constancy during the absence of Dr. Kane in the Arctic seas.

In New York, as elsewhere, Dr. Kane paid daily visits to Miss Fox, and often took her out for a drive. One day, having called, and heard that she had gone to visit some lady friends, he followed her to the house where the friends boarded, and entering the parlor, requested her to accompany him home. "Come, Maggie darling," he said, not seeming to heed the persons present.

Their engagement of course was not concealed from the near relations of Mrs. Fox. Some disturbance was caused by ill-timed advice and interference. While protesting his solemn determination

to marry Margaret Fox, Dr. Kane was equally
resolved that she should first complete her education.
He was not willing to take into his family an untutored girl, leaving her, as he must, during the years
of his absence, with unformed habits, and tastes undi-
rected by mental culture. Miss Fox herself was
opposed to an immediate union with her lover; for
her pride was enlisted in her wish first to render herself worthy of association with his distinguished relatives. She was not in the least ambitious for herself;
and it will be seen in the letters of Dr. Kane how
unceasing were his efforts to inspire her with sufficient ambition to make her appreciate the elevated
position he had offered her as his wife. He saw that
she cared little for worldly distinction, and he feared
that her love for him was not strong enough to induce
her to give up all the novelty and fascination of a
life of continual frivolous excitement, for the hope at
some uncertain period of being his own; the interval
to be passed in retirement. He was a prey to constant anxiety on this account, and kept an uneasy
watch over her while she was surrounded by people
interested in spiritualism. Dr. Kane used every
method in his power to detach her from them, and
was accustomed playfully to say that by holding up
his hand he could learn if she had or had not obeyed
his instructions. This he said he had learned of a
conjuror who had been in the East Indies.

VII.

After the return of Mrs. Fox and her daughter to
New York, Dr. Kane was in Washington, and wrote
this letter:

[Dr. Kane to Miss Fox.]

"THURSDAY, April 8th, 1853.

"I am in Washington, dear Mag—and oh, how
lonely! Your absence changes everything. The
city looks like a forlorn village, and the people like
a crowd of ill-dressed pickpockets.

"If I jump into a carriage, I think of the dear
little partner of my drives. If I dine in an oyster-
cellar, I think of Francis and his chafing-dish sup--
pers, or Mrs. R——, and her 'sassengers.' Indeed,
dear Maggie, sick as I was, I passed a happy time in
Washington.

"It was there that you first learned to feel how
much and how truly I cared for you; there, too, that
you first gave me your confidence, and with it your
love.

"Just for the sake of old times, I visited Mrs. Sullivan's. Some stranger occupied the parlor in which
we had spent so many frolic hours; and the third
story room was as naked and desolate as its white-
washed walls. Even the garret looked sad and disconsolate.

*   *   *   *   *

"But when I went into the parlor and saw the looking-glass before which you had so often brushed that tumble-down head of yours, and the wardrobe from which had so often issued the mysterious sounds —I felt quite sad. The fact is, 'LY' cares more about you than you deserve.

"Here, thought I, here in this very room, did my little *priestess* achieve her triumphs. Here sat dear loveable *whispering Waddy* with his *mental* questions; and here cute, but well believing Tallmadge, with his sharp, cunning eye, but foolish, credulous brain. Here my little Maggie led them all by the nose; and hereupon I set up a devil of a thinking—as to whether this girl who could so lead others would ever be led by me, or whether I too was not a Waddy Thompson of another sort, and Maggie only cheating me in a different way? Maggie, he who sows the wind will reap the whirlwind; and I have done wrong by you, my own dear little Maggie—wrong,—not because I did not state to you that our love might end in disappointment—not because I did not honestly open your eyes to the difference of our positions; but wrong because I still stayed near you, teaching you to love me, and weakly forgetting that every minute made it harder for us to break our chains— golden though they were, dear darling, golden though they were!

"But now that the deed is done, and that you have

given me, as you really have, your heart, I owe you
an atonement; and truly, Mag, will I make it. You
shall never regret having known and cared for me.   I
will be a brother to you.

"Remember that I am pure and disinterested; and
that you have never had from poor *Ly* a word that
would not make you a nobler woman.

"Dear Maggie, let us try to do what is right, and
give me credit for unselfish love in whatever I may do
for you.

"Now all this long preaching is to tell you that I
have a prospect of a home for you.   I have applied
to an aunt of mine, who owns a large country estate,
and she has, like a dear good friend, consented to
make all the arrangements.   This will leave you free
from any chance of misconstruction.   Through her
influence I can get you a quiet yet cheerful home,
where you will be the *only* boarder, and where you
may have a governess, and a room, and a piano all to
yourself.   It is true, dear Mag, that this home will be
a plain country gentleman's; a man with moderate
means and a large family; but you will be all the
happier for that.   You will be to them only as a lady;
no one shall know, not even *my* relative, where the
money comes from.   You can pay them yourself and
they will look up to you.   Miss ——, your governess,
is as ugly as sin, but she is a very good girl, whom
you can do as you please with.   It is with her father,
a rough broad Scotchman, that you will live.

"Here then, Maggie, free to do as you please, surrounded by good plain people, not too grand for your
comfort, with *my own aunt* to talk and advise with
you if you want a friend—it seems to me that you
will have everything that you can desire. And, oh,
Mag, how pleasant it would be to me to see as my
reward that you become a *refined*, educated, consci-
entious woman. It will cost me money, dear darling,
but it will be nothing if you show yourself worthy of
my care.

"After spending the summer in this country home,
you can enter Madam Moulenard's, at Albany, and
make Mrs. Turner's the home of your vacations.

"I will in a couple of days mention this to your
mother with full explanations, names, etc., etc. She
must then decide. If 'yes,' I will take her and you
to the place, let you see it, and then return to New
York to make your arrangements. In the mean
time keep it a secret, but write instantly telling me
what you think, for I will not write to your mother
until I hear from you.

"Do think often of

"LY."

There was an evident purpose in the warnings conveyed in the following and other letters; viz. to show
the unavoidable result of a continuance in the spirit-

rapping association. Perhaps the Doctor really faltered, at times, in his resolution to be true to his chosen one, in view of the ridicule and odium such an association might bring on himself; certain it is that he dreaded the consequences of his engagement becoming known. Hence his cautions to Margaret to be careful of his reputation, etc.

[Dr. Kane to Miss Fox.]

"MY DEAR SWEET MAGGIE:—Night has come, and the hour which ushers in another day is chiming from the cracked bells of Washington. Yet I sit down to give you my regular record of remembrance, to show my little Maggie that she is not forgotten.

"Dear Mag, though you have not written to me, I am every day the same—that good-natured, careful, loving 'Ly,' whose only thought is how he may please, whose only hope that he may train you to ways of pleasantness and peace. Do, dear darling, be lifted up and ennobled by my love. Live a life of purity, and meet your reward in the respect of yourself, the praise of this world, and the blessings of Heaven.

"Waddy called on me to-day, as did Tallmadge; I was kind to both for your sake. Waddy talked much about you. He said that he feared for you, and spoke long and well upon the dangers and temptations of your present life. I said little to him other than my convictions ot your own and your sister's excellent character and '*pure simplicity ;*' for thus, Mag, I always talk of you. And it pained me to find that others viewed your life as I did, and regarded you as occupying an ambiguous position. Depend upon it, Maggie, no right-minded gentleman—whether he be believer or skeptic—can regard your present life with approval. Let this, dear sweet, make you think over the offer of the one friend who would stretch out an arm to save you. Think wisely, dear darling, ere it be too late.

"In a few weeks I will be away from you. 'Thick ribbed ice, sterner than warrior's steel' will separate me from you. Never again will you have an unselfish, honorable friend, whose heart pulsates in unison with your own, whose thoughts are devoted to your welfare.

"Maggie, you cannot tell the sadness that comes over me when I think of you. What will become of you? you the one being that I regard even before myself! *Circumstance*, that tyrant of human destinies, forbids our marriage, except by a sacrifice of all that makes *worldly* life desirable; and to the gratification of our love we have the opposition of society, of education, and of conscience. Yet I tremble at the idea of bidding you good-bye for ever. The very thought of never returning fills me with indescribable awe and melancholy. Yet I feel that I ought never to see you again. Your love should die away with absence; and our continual meetings only add fuel to the flame.

Do write to me, Maggie, and tell me what your own heart tells you is best.

"If you really can make up your mind to abjure the spirits, to study and improve your mental and moral nature, it may be that a career of brightness will be open to you; and upon this chance, slender as it is, I offer, like a true friend, to guard and educate you. But, Mag, shadows, clouds, and darkness rest upon the execution of your good resolves; and I sometimes doubt whether you have the firmness of mind to carry them through.

"Last night, after writing to you, I held up my hand. Forgive me, Maggie, but I did not look back. I only tried to see what would be your future life. Oh, Maggie, Maggie, Maggie, how much misery I saw ahead! how much of bitter remembrance, of horrible regret! Yet with all this there was sunshine, and a voice sounded continually in my ears—Open to her the light—let her see the blessings of day, and she will not walk in darkness.

"Excuse this preaching letter. You know I am a queer mixture of good and bad. Therefore let me end with a Washington kiss and my love to Miranda.*

"LY.

"FRIDAY."

* "Miranda" was a poetical name assumed by the fair Maggie.

5

The reader will not fail to notice, in the continual complaints made by the lover of the young lady's coldness, and in the tone of her letters, that her affec tion at this time was far less demonstrative than his own.   She was very young, and unskilled in the expression of either feelings or thoughts, especially in letters.   There is a school-girl constraint about all she wrote at this period.   More than this; the extreme reserve which had been imposed by her few months of professional life, and her consciousness that the slightest unguardedness might subject her to undue familiarity, induced a degree of self-control, and a sensitive regard to her own dignity, which may easily have seemed like coldness to an impetuous admirer. She and others testify that never, in the whole course of her acquaintance with Dr. Kane, did he once forget the respect due to her, or overstep the limits of perfect decorum in his conduct towards her.   On the con- trary, he held her as something too pure and sacred for even an unhallowed thought.   She was in his eyes a divinity, enshrined in virtue's holiest sanctuary, and not to be gazed on by the vulgar crowd.   It was his greatest grief that she should be exposed to the intrusions of coarse and stupid persons, who frequented the spiritual circles.   Had not his Polar wanderings been before him, and had he been master of his own movements, he would doubtless have snatched her from such a life, by making her his wife at once.   But this could not be and meanwhile, he could not but

feel that her family consented with reluctance to part
with her, and that she herself hardly yet looked on
spiritual matters as he wished her to do. Hence his
warnings and reproaches; his cautions, and frequent
inconsistencies. Hence his assumption of the tone of
a mentor, and the comparisons of her social position
with his own, which may at times have piqued her
self-love.

In a letter addressed to a lady who had dared to
express some doubt of his honorable intentions towards
Miss Fox, he says :

[Dr. Kane to Mrs.——.]

"—— Your interest in my friend Maggie is the only
thing that could excuse a suspicion so gross and unkind
as that conveyed by your remarks. On this account
only I can make allowances for that spirit of distrust
which an experience of the deceit and hypocrisy of
those around us is but too apt to impart."

He alluded to the cruel suspicions of this lady in a
subsequent letter to Margaret, which shows how very
deeply he was wounded.

It may be necessary to explain also the desire of
concealment on Dr. Kane's part, and the stratagems
he proposed to enjoy the society of his beloved. The
relative under whose partial charge and in whose
house Miss Fox was then living, expected her at times
to join the circles as a medium, and was jealous of any

influence that took away her attention from spiritualism, or prejudiced her against it. The Doctor was
always fearful of giving offence, and preferred a little
artifice now and then, which did not always meet with
Miss Maggie's approval. With commendable discretion, she was ever determined to avoid anything
clandestine.

It would have been natural, too, had the changeful
tone of her lover's letters, and his occasional reproofs,
rendered her sometimes disposed to a little reticence,
beyond what might have been, had their love

> "Grown in the world's approving eyes,
>   In friendship's smile, and home's caress,
> Collecting all the heart's sweet ties
>   Into one knot of happiness."

Thus, she seems to have been sparing of her epis-
tolary favors. In the following missive, Dr. Kane
ironically expresses his obligation for "numerous letters"—— by way of reproaching her for her silence.

[Dr. Kane to Miss Fox.]

"MY DEAR MAGGIE:—The mail is closing, and
after a hard-working day, I have barely time to show
you that I remember you by writing my usual letter.

"Let me thank you for the numerous letters which
you have written during my absence. A letter is
always a proof that you exist in the thoughts of the
writer—and the letters which have so constantly

cheered the loneliness of poor *Ly*, show him how well he is remembered.

" When you write *again*, address Philadelphia, as I leave Washington to-morrow.

"I have attended, dear darling, to your interests; written to my aunt, and made all the necessary arrangements.   *   *   * 's conversation still annoys me; but I will do everything for you that a brother could do for a sister.

"I think it probable that I may write to your mother to come on by the Wednesday train of two o'clock P. M., to see the place. She will bring you with her, and if you are satisfied, and determined to adhere to your good resolves,—you can return to New York, and make your preparations to be back and housed in your new home by the first of May.

"There, dear Maggie, you will be a *lady;* your own mistress, and a person regarded with respect by the whole house. It shall be distinctly understood that you go or stay just as you please ;—for I am not going to turn 'preacher,' and bind up my little Maggie by a set of *rules*. I *trust* in you, and I feel that my confidence will never be abused. I will write at once, and arrange matters. Write to Philadelphia.

"NATIONAL HOTEL,

"April 11th, 1853.

"Good-bye, Pet Lamb."

The next was written on the same day:

"April 11th, NATIONAL.

"MY DEAR DARLING, who don't love me, and never writes to me, I leave Washington to-morrow (Tuesday afternoon) and reach Philadelphia that night, remaining a few days before going to New York.

"Now, I want you and your mother to start from New York on Wednesday morning. I will meet you both at the boat and Union Hotel, and on Thursday take you to Mrs. Turner's, where you can see your new home. If you cannot stay in Philadelphia till Sunday evening, I'll return with you; but I hope that you may be able to stay a couple of days in our dear old town.

"Bring some nice sleeves and undershirts, and a nice plain black frock, and plain bonnet; you are my child now!! I do hope my aunt will take a fancy to you. I never dreamt that I could so soon bring my little spirit-rapper into my family!

"Write at once to Philadelphia the hour of your leaving New York. With my regards to Mrs.——and your mother, I am your friend,

"PREACHER."

The ladies did not accept this invitation, nor did they see Mrs. Turner before the 27th of May.

VIII.

It was a favorite and oft-repeated expression with the Doctor,—"Maggie, you are a godsend to me!" With all his complaints of her shortcomings, he felt it an unspeakable happiness to love her, and to look for the unfolding of a responsive devotion in her young heart.

Dr. Kane was very often in the habit of saying— as if with melancholy presentiment—"What would become of you if I should die? What would you do? I shudder at the thought of my death, on your account."

In the buoyant confidence of youth, the poor girl could not then understand his fears. But *he* knew that in separating her from spiritualism he was isolating her from all her friends and associates, and depriving her of the only means she possessed of earning a livelihood. In compensation for the sacrifices required of her, he was giving her a hope only; a hope that might be blissfully realized, but might be sadly disappointed; and in the event of losing him, what must be her destiny!

This little note appears to have been written on the way from Washington.

" DEAR DARLING MAGGIE :—It is pleasant even to write your name again; but why no letters? Why no letters?

"I have just returned from hard work, in Washington, and am sick, worn out, thin as a lath, and very weary.

"Bye-bye, darling."

———

The following preceded Dr. Kane's return to New York.

"DEAR DARLING:—I know you think of me now. You miss my daily visits, my welcoming kiss, and the look which always followed you, trying to anticipate your wishes. You miss the dear stolen hours, the thoughts always bent upon your happiness. You miss our long rides, and our quiet little dinners; and now of all the so-called friends who surround you, there is not one on whose shoulder you could place your head and say, 'You love me for myself.' Therefore, dear Maggie, I know that you must think of me—*me*, the *only* human being that you can trust; the only heart before whom you are not wearing a perpetual disguise. Why, you must love me!

" Whatever may be my faults, I have at least loved you. Were you an empress, darling Maggie, instead of a little nameless girl, following an obscure and *ambiguous* profession, it would be the same. You could not have more from me.

" Is the old house dreary to you? Are the poor people below awaiting you, like Kennedy of old? Oh, Maggie, are you never tired of this weary, weary sameness of continual deceit? Are you thus to spend your days, doomed never to rise to better things?—you and that dear little open-minded sister Kate (for she too is still unversed in deception)—are you both to live on thus for ever? You will neither of you be happy if you do; for you are not, like * * * able to exult and take pleasure in the simplicity of the poor simple-hearted fools around you.

" Do then, Maggie, keep true to your last promise. Show this to Katy, and urge her to keep to her resolution.*

" Darling, I am very careful of you—more careful than you are of yourself. This is the last time I will ever allude to the ' rappings ' in a letter; but my friend (Cornelius Grinnell) has promised me to put it into your hands, and I feel that it is safe. You had better not mention the subject in your own letters, *unless they are put into his hands by yourself;* and do

---

* Miss Kate had promised to abjure the spirits, too, and go to live with her sister on her marriage with Dr. Kane.

burn or scratch out such parts of this letter as you would not have seen.

"You know I am nervous about the 'rappings.' I believe the only thing I ever was afraid of was, this *confounded thing being found out.* I would not know it myself for ten thousand dollars.

"My friend Mr. —— is very curious to know why I watched the house, and why Kate went to Philadelphia. I told him simply of a quarrel, or some such thing, between Mrs. —— and your mother; that you are all not very cordial, and will perhaps not stay very long in Twenty-sixth street. He wrote to me to-day, saying that Mrs. —— 'really surprised him.' He is half inclined to believe. Oh, Maggie, 'tis a d——d shame! Take care of yourself.

"God bless you!

"PREACHER."

————

The next letter, written in New York, refers to the visitors who came to witness the spiritual manifestations in Twenty-sixth street. Although, by this time, Margaret was as averse to sitting in circles as her lover could wish her to be, she was subjected to the associations she disliked while residing in the house. She has always averred that she never fully believed the rappings the work of spirits, but imagined some occult laws of nature concerned.

[Dr. Kane to Miss Fox.]

" MAGGIE DEAREST :—I am mad, angry, *disgusted*, at the hogs who have kept me from you on this my last day! What a life to lead—at the call of any fool who chooses to pay a dollar and command your time!

"Do you know, dear ' Ugly,' that I dreampt about you all night? You are a sad tempter, dear Maggie, but I intend to make you love me; and to do that you will always have from me confidence and respect.

" Perhaps, if you do not leave until Monday, I can yet see you again; for I will leave New York on Saturday, and give up every thing for the pleasure of seeing you again. Write to me, mailing your letter before ten, or nine o'clock, to-night. Direct to Delmonico's; and if you say so, I will come back and ride with you on Sunday.

"Maggie, think of me whenever you can, but do not think me a *fool*. I know you down to the very tips of your little feet. I know you better than a thousand Mrs. ——s! If you choose really to love me, I will give you a chance; if not, dear, darling Maggie, why, I'll care as little for you as you do for me.

" Accept; then, my respect; and remember that I look upon you as loving me *sincerely*. As long as you do this, you have in return from me every thing that I could give a most treasured friend.

"1 P. M."

IX.

Not long after this period, Dr. Kane was attacked with illness, while he was a guest at the house of Mr. Henry Grinnell, in Bond street, New York. How he longed to see his Maggie, may appear from what he wrote to her.

[Dr. Kane to Mrs. Fox.]

"DEAR MAGGIE :—Too sick to write, I am at Mrs. G——'s, and would dearly love to have you to nurse me, but fear that they would call your innocent devotion by another name. So write every day. I take a great comfort in your letters."

———

[Dr. Kane to Miss Fox.]

"DEAREST MAGGIE :—Tell my friend how and when we can write to each other ; as also all your movements.

"Be careful not to mention me before the Tigress, and do not talk to —— too much in her presence. You had better write a note at once to him with *directions*, and another, sealed, to me. Ever, dearest Maggie, the

"PREACHER.

"Love to Kate."

"MY SWEET MAGGIE :—I cannot see you to-day,
nor indeed can I tell when fate will enable me to see
you. I am very sick—for once down in bed, racked
by pains, and hardly able to trace these lines. Worse
than that, I am giving trouble to kind friends, and a
nuisance to all around me.

"It is in sickness that I feel how dear you are to
me—how truly, warmly, and honestly I would watch
and love you. Twice has the carriage driven to the
door, and poor Ly made a fruitless effort to get into
it; but in vain. I can only think of you, and long
for the gentle eyes and warm kisses which would do
so much more for me than the doctors. Maggie, if
you have any heart at all, do write me a long, loving
letter!

"Make yourself easy about ——'s matter. I
understand why you want it carefully confined to
yourselves, and have bound up Mr. G——, so as to
make him safe. Maggie, let me give you a piece of
advice: '*Always believe and trust me.*' You were
foolish in telling Mr. G—— about that thing, because
he said that *I* had told him. *I* have never told him.
He said untruly when he told you so. When will
you learn to trust me? Never!!

"Pet lamb, in a few days we part: I on my ardu-
ous track—you to the quiet enjoyment of a happy
home. Are we ever to meet again? Are we to walk

arm in arm over sunny fields—to gaze at Italian sun-
sets from lofty mountains? Are we ever to be more
to each other than we now are? Or is this—our
soon-coming farewell—to be eternal?

"Answer me in your note, direct and to the point.
Don't be afraid of writing, for I will return the letter.
Say to me, dear darling, shall I bind myself? and I
will send you to-morrow a binding letter. But oh,
dear Mag, give me some written assurance that you
will do the same. Show trust and faith, for without
it you will never retain my love.

"I'm very sick, dear Maggie. Do take your time,
and answer me—by the bearer.

"Morton will call to-morrow, and tell you how I
am."

The next day came the following:

[Dr. Kane to Miss Fox.]

"DEAR MAGGIE:—Read my yesterday's letter again,
and you will perhaps find something unanswered.

"My darling, I am very sick—the doctor says so,—
Don't mention this to your people; but say I am too
busy to call. Were I still at the hotel, I would send
for you to nurse me; but Mrs. G——, at whose house
I now am, would not understand my little Maggie, of
whom I try to be as careful as a sister.

"I suffer so much, dear pet, that I cannot write.
If you have anything to do, and don't feel like writing

do not write.   I don't want to bore you.   I will never
give a speck of trouble to my Mag, if I can help it,
nor will I be angry ; so do, dear darling, do just as
you please.   I know that you love me, and that
is enough.

"I hate people who pester me for letters, and I
don't want you to hate me.

"Bye bye !   I'm very sick."

Miss Margaret wrote as follows :

[Miss Fox to Dr. Kane.]

"MY DEAR LY :—Are you no better?   I fear
you are not.   I wish I could hear from you every
hour !   I suppose your mother is with you now.   Do
come here as soon as you are able to ride out.   You
ask if you shall write 'a binding letter'—no—dear
Ly—your word is enough.

"All I ask for my dear Ly is that you may get
well.   I am so glad your mother is with you.   Do let
me hear from you as often as possible.

"In haste, yours,
"MAGGIE.

"Shall I send those letters back to Mr. Grinnell ?'
(Dr. Hawks's letters.)

[Dr. Kane to Miss Fox.]

"MAGGIE DARLING :—I am really sick—too sick
to think of those who are nursing me, except as kind

and devoted friends. My mother has been sent for, and will be here to-morrow. My one thought is yourself. Do, my own dear love, lift up, and refine yourself, and hurry on your preparations, so as to leave as soon as you can; for, whatever may happen, you shall be cared for."

[Dr. Kane to Miss Fox.]

"MY OWN SWEET MAGGIE:—Ly is very sick; so sick that you must make up your mind not to see him for a long time. All my people have been sent for, and are here. If you want to show me that you care for me, write me at *least* one long affectionate letter.

"Return to me Dr. Hawks' papers. I can just trace these lines.

[Dr. Kane to Miss Fox.]

"See Mr. Grinnell, sick or well.

"DEAREST MAGGIE:—How grieved I am that you should be sharing my troubles, and down yourself upon a sick bed! I long to see you, and the first liberty will see me at your side. Keep up your spirits, dear pet lamb.

"If you are able to ride out to-morrow between twelve and four P. M., you can easily call on me, with Kate or your mother. I told Mrs. G—— that you had offered to ask 'the spirits' some questions as to my recovery, and she is very *curious* to see the performance. So, dear Maggie, if you will gladden my eyes—say so in writing (not mentioning it to Mr. G——) and I will send a carriage. Name the exact hour, and don't keep it waiting,—for Mrs. G —— will send her own carriage. Keep this a secret from Mrs. ——

"God bless my sweet Maggie!"

[Dr. Kane to Miss Fox.]

"DEAR PET:—If you and Kate can name any day, between ten and half-past three, I can see you here. Mrs. G —— is very anxious to hear 'a knock proceed from me'—and a visit would be very cheering to poor 'Ly.' She will send her carriage for you; only write me the time, and be plainly dressed, awaiting it. Oh, how I long to see you! Get well, dear darling, if only to make happy your faithful friend, who will ever guard you."

[Dr. Kane to Miss Fox.]

" So, after an illness of nearly a fortnight, I send a carriage for you, and receive the answer 'cannot possibly come.' Your affections must be very oppressive;—your trouble at my sickness very unendurable! 'Can't possibly come!' You do me too much honor, Miss Margaret Fox!

Well, Ly won't get mad: He can't. He loves you too much; but if ever God spares him to traverse the Arctic ice, and he thinks of you in your quiet country home, it will be with the comfortable feeling of conviction that you won't suffer from your *Love* for him. No, Maggie! You'll never die of too much heart!

"Don't rap for Mrs. Pierce (the wife of the President of the United States). Remember your promise to me. A promise my hand has just told me has been *twice* broken within these forty-eight hours. How much oftener I don't know.

"Begin again, dearest Maggie, and keep your word. No rapping for Mrs. Pierce, or evermore for any one. I, dear Mag, am your best, your truest, your only friend. What are they to my wishes? Oh, regard and love me, and listen to my words; and be careful, very careful, lest in an idle hour you lose my regard and your own respect.

"The carriage shall call for you to-morrow. You need not rap; I had rather you would not. Receive this note kindly and write me an answer, for although my hands let me write, I am very, very sick."

The above seems to have elicited a brief reply, which was noticed as follows:

[Dr. Kane to Miss Fox.]

" DEAR SWEET :—Don't trouble yourself. I could not be angry if I was to try. I'm very sick, but think of you constantly. Morton will come up every day. Do have sometimes a kind note for poor Ly.

" Bye bye."

———

Some time afterwards this note was written.

[Dr. Kane to Miss Fox.]

" DEAR MAGGIE :—I am delighted at the chance of seeing you. Come alone, if Kate cannot accompany you.

" Treat me like a dear brother, without reserve or formality ; and do not see them until you see me.

" Do have neat neck and arm linen, and believe always and everywhere in the confiding love of

" LY."

———

The carriage waited till the young lady, usually dilatory in dress matters, was ready ; and she was received with a cordial welcome by Mrs. Grinnell. The Doctor was lying on a couch, wearing a robe of crimson stuff. The sight of her he loved revived his spirits. He bade his kind hostess show the young lady various little objects of curiosity; among them a curious mechanical contrivance by which a little bird of gorgeous plumage was made to fly out, plume its feathers, trill a song, and retire. "If that belonged to me," whispered Dr. Kane to Margaret, "it should be yours." They talked then a long while about her going to school and the various studies she was to pursue. Mrs. Grinnell, as Dr. Kane afterwards said, was very much pleased with his young visitor.

X.

[Dr. Kane to Miss Fox.]

"DEAR MAGGIE :—Not so well this morning, but very glad to have seen again the light of your eyes.

"Do not think, darling, that I don't love and trust you ; but you require a little scolding now and then.

"Tell me how Mrs. Pierce got on !

"Mrs. Grinnell was much pleased with you. Every body who really knows you, *is;* for my Maggie is a *lady ;* and by the time that she has had a course of Mrs. Turner's music and French, nobody will know her as the spirit-rapping original phenomenon.

"Write me daily. Bye bye."

To explain the allusion to Mrs. Pierce, it may be mentioned that the wife of the President had made an engagement to call on Miss Fox, at the request of Governor Tallmadge and other friends in Washington.

————

[Dr. Kane to Miss Fox.]

"MY DEAR DARLING :—Your sweet note did me as much good as a dozen doctors. Do write again. I've been and am still very sick; but my hands let me write again.

"Always have faith in me, dear Maggie, and you shall never regret it. Once distrust, and you have no claim on Ly. Glad that your bird sings so well."

———

Several notes like the following were written during his convalescence.

[Dr. Kane to Miss Fox.]

"DEAR MAGGIE:—I am really sick, but the day is so charming that I think a ride will do me good.

"Will not you and Kate jump in, and I will try and give you both a happy day!

"Don't disappoint me, but hurry.

"Give my respects to Mrs. —— and tell her I am sorry that I was unable to see her last night."

———

The allusion to the rappings in this note to Miss Kate is a mere joke, for the Doctor *never* countenanced them by experiments.

[Dr. Kane to Miss Kate Fox.]

"MISS KATE FOX :—A carriage will call for you and Miss Maggie at one o'clock. Can your spirits thump in a carriage? If they cannot, I would rather come up and have the *rappings* elsewhere.

"Do not disappoint me. I have some important test questions. At one precisely.

"YOUR FRIEND."

——

[Dr. Kane to Miss Fox.]

"DEAR MAGGIE :—I send you a carriage; perhaps Kate or Mrs. —— will take an airing. After you have had about an hour's ride the driver will call for me, and I will join you, and return to spend the evening.

"Your friend,
"E. K. KANE."

——

The observations on persons in these letters are usually quite harmless, but must occasionally be omitted, that the feelings of none may be wounded.

"MY SWEET PET:—I send your letters. Is there anything else that poor sick *Ly* can do for you ? * * * * * * * * *

I can't be *playing a part* before *you.*

"Dont forget, dear Mag, the *lock* and the sweet long letter. Have it at Bond Street before five o'clock P.M.

"If you can go to the theatre with Kate, send word by bearer on a scrap of paper, and I'll have a box for you and a carriage at half-past six P.M. Do go, dear darling ! If you prefer to-morrow, say so, and I'll call *to-night* and see my little bird.

"Maggie, dear, I want you, if you possibly can, to go to the theatre to-night. The day is so dreary and I feel so badly that I long for a long talk with you. Tell Kate to go, and let me call for you in a carriage at a quarter before seven o'clock this evening. Do, dear Mag!"

" DEAR KATY :—Will you go to the theatre to-night with Mr. G., your sister, and myself?

"I have not seen you for three days. I hope you are not angry with your friend

"PREACHER.

"I have a nice private box for you."

" MAGGIE DARLING :—All last night did this good
friend of yours think about you and your probable
future.

" I can see that this is one of the turning points of
your life, and upon your own energy and decision
now depend the success and happiness of your future
career. Dear Maggie, think it over well, and do not
be turned aside from what is right by the sincere but
still misguided advice of others.

" I know, dear pet, that the life has its attractions.
There is a real enjoyment in the excitement of watching and working for the conversion of the skeptical.
Do not think, then, that poor 'Ly' blames you for
this natural fondness for the *ingrown* habits of six
years. But remember, Maggie, that all this will not last.
It is '*fun*' now, but what will it be six years hence!
What will it be when, looking back upon *twelve* mis-
spent and dreary years, you feel that there have been
no acts really acceptable to your Maker, and that, for
the years ahead, all will be sorrow, sameness, and
disgust! Dear, sweet Maggie, think it over well.

" There is but one *life* in this world—*that of self-
approval.* There is but one happiness—that of loving
and being loved. Where will you meet either of
these, living as you now live?

" Why, you know that sometimes even now, when
—— is cross, or the company coarse and vulgar, or

6

the day tiresome, or yourself out of sorts, that low spirits and disgust come over you, and you long like a bird to spread your wings and fly away from it all. Dear, sweet pet, I am going soon far away—never, perhaps, to see you again ; certainly *never* as a *spirit-rapper*. Do, darling, while you can, spread your wings, fly away, and be at rest.

"God bless you!"

[Dr. Kane to Miss Fox.]

"DEAR MAGGIE:—I thought of you all day, dreampt of you nearly all night, and now in the bright morning time am thinking of you still. Don't be discouraged, my dear darling ; things will be right again. *Ly* will not desert you, and this temporary cloud will pass away.

"The more I think of it, the more I am convinced that I did right in speaking of your affair to Mrs. ——. She misconstrued my motives, and replied by insult. Yet I did as a gentleman ought ; and now, conscious of my rectitude of intention, I feel as if I had but one duty—that of guarding your interests and watching over your happiness. Although I cannot enter her doors, I will never forget the dear friend who, reposing confidence in my word, looks to me as to one who holds her happiness in his hands.

Trust me, dear Maggie, for I will guard you as a brother.

" Whatever you advise, I will do, and I await your answer by Grinnell. If you will permit me to speak about the arrangement for a *home* near Philadelphia, I will do it at once. Only write me your wishes. Banished as I am from you, no longer pressing your dear lips or watching your glad smile, I feel as if I could do any thing, resign any thing, to see you happy. Only say to me, dear darling, what you would have me do.

" I send my friend with this, to defend himself against the wicked insinuations of that woman. Maggie you know that I cannot tell a falsehood. Believe me, then, that if you were my own sister, you could not stand higher in his eyes than you do. I have told him of Mrs. ——'s accusations, and he is shocked that one whose character is so known as mine should be so assailed. Do, dear Maggie, have confidence in him. I have told him how much I regard you, and how dear to my wishes it would be to take your future path under my guidance.

" Maggie, I have tried to comfort you, but I am sad myself;—sad and sick. I miss that dear Maggie, with her glossy locks upon my shoulders; that wicked, teasing, spirit-rapping Maggie! Oh, dear, darling pet, when can I see you! I leave on Monday, and am nearly crazy at the idea of not bidding you good-bye. Yet I cannot go to ——'s unless she apologizes, and even then but once. Do try and see me. I leave it all to you. Write me word how and when, and I will faithfully meet you; but be careful, darling, for I would not harm you for the world.

"With God's blessing, in a week you shall be free; but, dear Maggie, you must help me. *Never*, from this hour, the raps again! Never, dear Mag, never!

"As to ——, she is to you no legal guardian. Your mother is everything. If I do my duty, and you stand firm, all will be right.

"Bye bye!

"'Ly.'

"Do not tell any one that I leave on Monday for Philadelphia. It will have a good effect to let them think me in town, and staying away."

XI.

All this time Dr. Kane had talked with Mrs. Fox about sending Margaret to school during the years of his contemplated absence, and had at length obtained her consent to this cherished project.   The only thing now necessary was to select the school.   General Waddy Thompson wrote to recommend one; and a journey was projected to New Haven to enquire about schools in that classic locality; one there having been highly recommended by Bishop ——. The Doctor's plan of private schooling under the care of his aunt, seems not to have been at first approved by Mrs. Fox, perhaps because it would remove Margaret to a distance from all her friends.

As soon as Dr. Kane was sufficiently recovered, he made arrangements for this journey.   He wrote:

[Dr. Kane to Miss Fox.]

"DEAR MAG:—I will have a carriage for you punctually between four and half-past four.   Bring Kate with you, and do not disappoint your friend; for I will call for you in person.

"Tell your mother that on Wednesday we will leave for New Haven; and do urge upon her the importance of hastening your school arrangements. I am deeply anxious to see you fixed finally before

I leave; and my time, dear child, is fully occupied.

"You know now how brotherly my feelings are, and how pleasant it would be to me—when floating in that Arctic waste—to feel that I had contributed to make your life useful and happy.

"At present you have nothing to look forward to —nothing to hope for. Your life is one constant round of idle excitement. Can your mother—who is an excellent woman—look upon you, a girl of thirteen, as doomed all your life to live surrounded by such as now surround you—deprived of all the blessings of home, and love, and even self respect?

"Do hasten and go to school; study hard, and be a useful woman; an honor to your mother and yourself."

———

Once he said, playfully,—"You know not what a great man is your 'Lish!'" and went on to tell Maggie how he had breakfasted with Queen Victoria when he was in England. He had an object in wishing to increase her respect for himself, inasmuch as a powerful influence was needed to separate her from all her associates.

———

The following note to Mrs. Fox was in relation to the visit to New Haven.

"MY DEAR MADAM:—The cars leave for New Haven at eight A. M., and return early in the afternoon, reaching New York by nine in the evening.

"This will leave but a few hours for business, and I will have to work hard to complete the arrangements.

"Tell the young ladies that I will have a carriage for them punctually at seven o'clock, Monday morning, and that they had better be all ready, so as not to delay. They can pick me up on their road to the cars.

"Very truly,
"Your servant,
"E. K. KANE.

"MRS. FOX."

———

"DEAR MAGGIE:—Your wishes are with me always binding. I do not think that you can look back upon a wish ungratified, when your friend had it in his power to grant it; therefore, darling, of course, bring your mother.

"The carriage will be with you at seven A. M. If

Katy would go, there would be no impropriety, and I have often said that I take the same care of you that I would of my own sister. Do therefore exactly as you please.

"God bless you!

"YOUR FRIEND.

"Answer by bearer."

Mrs. Fox determined to accompany her daughter and Dr. Kane to New Haven. Another missive to Miss Margaret kept her in mind of the hour of starting.

[Dr. Kane to Miss Fox.]

"Send me word what your mother says about the dog, as I have to give the man an answer by eight this evening. If you prefer a small lap-dog, or a hairy Newfoundland, let cousin Peter know, for your wishes are his laws.

"I have written to your mother, telling her to have you ready by seven A. M. We will have precious little time in New Haven. Would it not be well to tell your mother that we may come back by the boat? It is a beautiful journey along the Sound.

"Be assured that while with me *no accidents* can happen. I will not only be 'very good,' but I will make you 'good' too. There!

"Write me back a nice, long, loving letter, for I cannot see you to-day. That house is as hot as a furnace, and as uncongenial to a person of refinement, as a tallow candle, or a lump of *brown* soap.

"Especially mention in your letter if you will be ready at seven o'clock.

"Remember me to Kate, and ask my kind and considerate hostess if there is anything that I can send to Mr. —— *

"Always respect sickness, dear Maggie. It is God's bitter lesson; preaching to mortals their frail hold upon the dear blessings of life. No one in full health can realize the awful prospect of a sudden fall into the dark regions—of *true spirits*. Maggie, child, shun sin—shun hypocrisy; shun the 'preachers;'—injure not even the worm that crawls; but live and love, and be happy.

"Bye bye!"

————

The quest in New Haven was not very satisfactory. In one establishment burning-fluid was used—a very dangerous thing; and in another, none but an upper room could be procured. The Doctor declared he should not have a happy moment during his absence,

———
* The gentleman whose sickness is alluded to, was the husband of a relative of Mrs. Fox, residing in 26th street.

if his little girl were exposed to the perils of explosive compounds. Going into one institute, he made Maggie throw back her veil; he seemed always pleased at the admiration her innocent beauty awakened.

The subject of the school to be chosen was in agitation while Dr. Kane's last preparations for the Arctic Expedition were going on. Meantime, in view of the interference that had already caused some unhappiness, he urged Mrs. Fox not to heed what outsiders might say: but to depend implicitly upon his judgment, discretion, and honor. They would in time see how faithful he would be to the sacred trust. One day he came to the house, accompanied by his brother, and taking Mrs. Fox aside, requested her not to say a word about the marriage before that gentleman; while in his brother's presence he begged her not to let such a rumor get abroad in public, on her daughter's account; adding, "my brother feels like death about it."

———

The following note was sent immediately after the decease of the relative already mentioned:

[Dr. Kane to Miss Fox.]

"DEAR MAG:—I send Morton to you, deeply regretting that I cannot come in person to cheer your sadness. I shall not leave for Philadelphia to-morrow, as I cannot bear to leave you in your distress.

"E. K. KANE."

———

It may be mentioned that Mr. Morton was the confidential friend and faithful follower of Dr. Kane, and the companion of his Arctic travels. He was highly regarded by Miss Maggie, whom he looked on with the deepest respect.

Dr. Kane called upon the family very soon afterwards. While standing with Margaret, her sister, and others, in the room where the corpse was lying—moved by a sudden impulse—he took the hand of his beloved, and called those present to witness his solemn vow and promise that she should be his wife on his return from the Polar seas; "I will be true to you"—he said, "till I am as the corpse before you," requiring a similar pledge from her. He seemed, at times, to feel that the bond between them needed this kind of seal, as the engagement could not be publicly known. A little jealousy—too, is perceptible on his part. This solemn pledge is presently referred to.

This portion of a letter breathes a moralizing spirit —shadowed by the near approach of the parting hour.

———

* * "What gold can equal the self-approval of a good conscience! And what are we, dear Mag, when, looking back upon the silent years, memory lingers upon no good deeds done, and a profitless and dreary old age stands before us like a spectre!

"Be true to yourself, and even as a loved brother I will be true to you, until I am as the corpse before you.

* * "I have never yet left a wish of yours ungratified, and if I can help it, never will. You therefore may decide for me. Shall I go or stay?"

["Shall I go or stay?" was often his question to Maggie, on the eve of any important movement. He left to this simple girl the decision of the most remarkable acts of his life, sure that she would decide with a disinterested view to his honor and happiness.]

"It is hard to leave you, when death has taken away an early friend, and still harder, dear Mag, to feel that you will be left to solitude and your own sad thoughts. Still I feel as if it was my duty to go —and I know that my dear, well-trusted little Maggie will not counsel me to do wrong.

"I will call upon you again to-morrow, exactly at twelve."

[Dr. Kane to Miss Fox.]

"DEAR MAGGIE:—It was of little use my staying to see you, for I am worse to-day, and the doctor will not let me leave my room.

"Keep up your spirits, dear darling, and expect to see me to-morrow; for I will not leave you in your sorrow.

"Read over my yesterday's letter, and profit by its counsels. Do, dear Mag, take advantage of this *death*, to renew your good intentions. Write me a letter, solemnly promising never to rap again. Do, dear Mag, do this; you will feel happier for it. Remember in this awful hour of death the fearful sins and sorrows that have grown out of that girlish trick. Think how the little stream has become a mountain torrent; and when the great God punishes, He will go to the fountain-head. Do, do, dear Pet, make me the promise."

This appeal met with a prompt response—as appears from the following missive; though few copies of Miss Margaret's letters belonging to this period were preserved by her.

[Dr. Kane to Miss Fox.]

"DEAR MAG:—Your kind promise 'solemnly never to rap again' so pleases me that I cannot help thanking you. Adhere to that, and you will be a dear, good, happy girl, and secure in me a valued friend.

"Cheer up, dear Mag. I am not going to bore you with any more sermons. It is better for poor C—— that he be in the silent tomb than fighting the grim enemy with pain and sorrow. He died a believer in the spirits, and taking comfort in his delusion: and we who live will profit by his death, that our own *belief* may be no chimera, but a hope and a blessing.

"What's the use of fretting! In a few days you will be surrounded by new scenes in your quiet country home. There will be plenty of people around you to whom you can extend little charities, and lay up a stock of pleasant recollections to wipe out the past. I should laugh to see you—'Devil,' as I often call you—trudging about among the cottages, blowing children's noses, and giving sugar-candy to the babies. I must get you a large dog, and you can take Tommy with you.

"Keep up your spirits. I will come and see you— God willing—to-morrow. In the meantime eat some of these nice brandy plums: they will cheer you up.

"Some day or other—Polar ice permitting—we will thaw out in Italy. Dear, sweet Italy! land of sunshine and flowers, and music and lovers! Looking from some high mountain down upon tranquil plains; you shall forget that you ever cheated old fogy Waddy Thompson, or rubbed your nose red for poor C——.

"Cheer up! Bye bye.

"Am I not a good fellow! sick and sad, thus to write and comfort my little Mag!"

XII.

The family of Mrs. Fox went to Rochester accompanying the remains of Mr. ——. While they were there this letter was received from the Doctor.

"MY DEAR MAGGIE:—You were right in going to Rochester. It was your duty to gratify the wish of Mrs. ——. Never think that I will not sanction a kind or a just act.

"Your letter fills me with satisfaction. Your present tone of mind is what I have longed for, and I know that it will please you to have my approval. I do not often praise you; regard it, therefore, as something beyond mere words, when I say that you are doing right; and if you adhere to your good resolves will surely have your reward.

"No matter for the *churches*, Maggie. Live a life of purity and innocence, making those around you happy; and the *Great God*, whose mandate is ' Love one another,' will love you. Many happy years are ahead of you to wipe out the memory of the past; and surely it is worth something to have the support and regard of one steadfast friend like myself.

"You say truly that life is not long at the longest; therefore, dear Mag, seize the sunshine while it lingers, and make the most of its fleeting hours. You know my opinions often expressed to you, that good deeds are the best offerings to the 'Great Author of Good,' and that if we lead a life which injures no one around us, which has for its aim making others happy, dispensing charities and covering our footsteps with blessings, such a life will have its reward, church or no church.

"Believe me when I say we were not placed in this bright world to wear long, solemn faces, and turn up our noses at its enjoyments and pleasures. To live, to *love*, to *enjoy*, are parts of the great religion of *Gratitude*, which tells us to take of the good things of this world: for '*to-morrow ye die.*'

"Be happy then, dear Maggie; lean upon me, and so live as to meet *my* approval. You will be then sure of your *own*, and your path will be strewn with flowers.

"I cannot promise not to hold up my hand again, but I will not do so for some time. I confess that I was deeply pained by what my hand told me for the past fortnight in connexion with ——; but I never said so to you. Judge, then, how glad I was to get your solemn promise. Now I can trust and confide in you, for I know you will not deceive me, nor break a pledge given in the presence of *Death*.

"Write to me to Philadelphia (under cover to my brother). Your letters marked 'Private,' *inside*. I am about the same, waiting for clear weather to return.

"Perhaps you had better send me a letter also to No. 17 Bond street. I do not leave New York till Monday."

Addressed to
MISS MAGGIE FOX, Rochester.

———

[Dr. Kane to Miss Fox.]

"DEAR MAGGIE:—Be in to-day at one o'clock, for I am going to make an effort to see you, and fix finally all your school matters.

"Yours always with my blessing,

"E. K. KANE."

———

[Dr. Kane to Miss Fox.]

"MY OWN DEAR MAGGIE:—Have you no feeling? Why do you not write to me? Surely you cannot distrust poor *Ly!*

"I leave to-morrow, and God only knows when I can see you again. If you can see me on Monday morning I should prefer it; for then I could go to Philadelphia by the two o'clock cars with my brother.

"Answer.

"I have told Mr. Grinnell to get from your mother

a positive answer—'yes or no'—to my hopes of providing you with a school and a home. I must have an answer when I see you; for I want either to fix matters or banish it for ever.

"Do, my own dearly loved Maggie, decide rightly, confiding in the purity of your only friend.

"Write me a long, loving letter, for I am sick and unhappy."

———

It was now settled that Maggie was to go to school at Crookville, and was to be under the charge of Dr. Kane's aunt, Mrs. Leiper, residing in the family of that lady's intimate friend and neighbor, Mrs. Turner. In the next letter Dr. Kane urges the hastening of preparations.

[Dr. Kane to Miss Fox.]

"DEAR MAGGIE :—If to-morrow be clear, and my poor body permit, I will call at half-past twelve to spend a parting half hour with you.

"I am going for a few days to Philadelphia—a visit for the restoration of my health. Do, dear darling, hasten your preparations, for I want to see you in your own home before I take my longer journey.

"Have you received your trunk? It was the finest that I could procure in New York. The 'Children

of the Abbey' will come to-morrow. Is there anything else, dear darling, that I can send you?

"I am not so well to-day—low-spirited and sad.
Will you do me a favor? As soon as Morton hands
you this, write me a dear, sweet, loving little letter,
and send with it a lock of your hair. It will soothe
me to sleep. Do this, dear Mag., and I'll try my best
merely to ' *like you*.'

"Bye bye."

"Send me word how you are. Mr. Grinnell will
probably call to-night. Do see him, dear Maggie.
Tell your mother to hasten your clothes, etc., etc., for
school."

[Dr. Kane to Miss Fox.]

" I was very glad, my own dearest darling, that you
contradicted the suspicions of my hand. My hand
is sometimes completely wrong, and I had a great
deal rather believe you than it. As long, dear Maggie, as you love me, I will care for you, and never
distrust you any more.

" Now that you are about to leave me, I begin to

feel how much I love you. How anxiously I desire your welfare! How tremblingly I look to your future course! Do not desert the memory of your true friend; for the time is at hand when you will see him no more. When raging seas and fearful ice will separate us, and a cold, cold winter freeze out the warmth of my thoughts.

"It would be very, very wicked, after what has passed, for you to cease to love me. I want you, dear Maggie, to respect yourself and be happy. You cannot do this if you consider my love like that of others, and desert your friend the

"—— PREACHER.

" Good-bye."

" I will call at three P.M., and either spend the evening or ride, as you and Kate may desire.

"Please yourself, and you will please me."

The little *jeu d'esprit* that follows was written just before the departure for school. It shows the opinion the Doctor just then entertained of the young lady's matter-of-fact character, contrasting it with his own romance and sentiment. She was always too refined and bashful, however, ever to say "confound it," or to use any such expressions as are imputed to her. These must be attributed to poetic licence.

Dialogue between the sentimental "PREACHER" *and practical* MAGGIE.

SCENE.—MRS. ——'s PARLOR.

1.

PREACHER.

Dearest, may thy life be gilded as the sunset sky !

MAGGIE.

I really think I'd like a "sassage;" hand me one, dear Ly.

PREACHER.

May thy thoughts be free from passion as an infant's dream !

MAGGIE.

There's a pin against your Maggie! Catch it, or I'll scream!

2.

PREACHER.

Maggie, I have watched the feelings welling in thy breast.

MAGGIE.

Confound this frock! it always slips, and leaves me
half undressed.

PREACHER.

I've often longed to make life's stream a fountain
clear and bright.

MAGGIE.

How can I fix my hair, dear Ly, if you stand in
the light?

3.

PREACHER.

And now I've found a rural home, away from toil
and strife.

MAGGIE.

Yes, and an ugly governess to lead me "such a life!"

PREACHER.

A home, my Maggie, where your heart and mind
will grow apace!

MAGGIE.

And nobody but country bumpkins come around
the place!

PREACHER.

A home of peace, where every thought can centre,
love, on me.

MAGGIE.

And sour old maids, and rainy days, and you
upon the sea!

> [*Exit* PREACHER *in a huff, and* MAGGIE
> *laughing as she sings out* "*Italy!*
> *Italy! Italy!*"]

Italy was often talked of as the country to which
the wedding trip should be made.

———

[Dr. Kane to Miss Fox.]

"MY DEAR MAGGIE:—Mr. Grinnell's conversation will show you that I have cared for you, and
kept all my promises.

"Write to me if Wednesday afternoon will do for
you to leave New York with your mother.

"Never do wrong any more; for if now the
spirits move,' it will be a breach of faith. From this
moment our compact begins.

"Bye bye. Your friend and brother,

"E. K. KANE."

———

In another note he says:

[Dr. Kane to Miss Fox.]

"I do not fear a dozen Argus-eyed ——s. It is because, dearest, I do not wish you to have a single pang in after years. I would not have you ever repent your relations with Ly. You are a child now, but there is darkness ahead. Let us both fight against it. Do not then feel sad; it is your interest alone that I would guard and cherish.

"And now, dear Maggie, should you grow very impatient to see your mother, and Mrs. Turner approves your having a few days' rest from your studies, write to Mr. Grinnell, and he will be your escort. Always confide in him; he is a gentleman.

" ☞ Remember!

" Bye bye.

" 'LISH."

———

Maggie was sitting for her portrait to Mr. Fagnani; a portrait which Dr. Kane made his inseparable companion in his Arctic wanderings. When toiling through the frozen wastes, he would not even permit Morton to carry for him this treasure; but bore it, in its frame, strapped on his back, wherever he went, and at night had it placed by his couch of rest.

7

The following was written on the twenty-sixth of May, 1853:

"DEAR MAGGIE:—You will sit with Mr. Fagnani until half-past three o'clock. Morton will then take you home, and your mother must be all ready to go at once with you to the cars. There you will meet me.

"On no account fail, for I can accompany you on no other day. Say this to your mother, and be all ready. Morton will not leave you till you see me.

"E. K. KANE."

Dr. Kane's practical wisdom did not prevent his sometimes showing a slight tendency to superstition. One day, taking a rosebud Maggie had given him, he bade her open her mouth to catch it; saying that if she did so, it would be an omen of his safe return, and of their wedded happiness. He then threw it to her, and was well pleased to have it caught. He did the same with a nut, on the eve of his departure for England, in October, 1856.

XIII.

The time grew fearfully short. The preparations of Mrs. Fox being completed, Dr. Kane escorted her and Margaret, on the twenty-sixth, as far as Philadelphia. They stopped at the Girard House, and supped together for the last time in years.

It was at their parting that Margaret first felt how deeply she loved the man who had shown such devotion to her—such tender care for her welfare. The anguish that followed his departure was intolerable; and she was on the point of giving up the idea of going to school, and returning to her friends in New York to seek relief from overwhelming distress. But this would have been an unkind return for the love lavished upon her. Mrs. Kemble's lines would have been applicable in her case :—

" What shall I do with all the days and hours
   That must be counted ere I see thy face!
How shall I charm the interval that lowers
   Between this time and that sweet time of grace!

    *   *   *   *   *

"I'll tell thee : for thy sake, I will lay hold
   Of all good aims, and consecrate to thee
In worthy deeds each moment that is told,
   While thou, beloved one! art far from me.

" For thee I will arouse my thoughts to try
    All heavenward flights, all high and holy strains;
For thy dear sake I will walk patiently
    Through the long hours, nor call their minutes pains.

" I will this dreary blank of absence make
    A noble task-time, and will therein strive
To follow excellence, and to o'ertake
    More good than I have won since yet I live.

" So may this doomèd time build up in me
    A thousand graces, which shall thus be thine;
So may my love and longing hallowed be,—
    And thy dear thought an influence divine."

————

On the twenty-seventh of May, after a melancholy
breakfast, Mrs. Fox and Margaret stepped into the
carriage engaged by Dr. Kane to convey them eighteen miles into the country, to the house of Mrs. Turner. The words of her lover—"It is too near our
parting"—had sunk deeply into the heart of the poor
girl, and it was almost with dismay, as she drew near
her future abode, she realized that—shut out from the
world in this retired spot—she had also lost the sun
of her heart's world: that she should no more hear
the voice of him she now loved with an ardor scarcely
less than that of his own attachment to her. The
clasp of his hand—his tender looks—how they lin-

gered in her memory! But it was a consolation to
think that in remaining here she was fulfilling his
dearest wish; that his aunt, to whose care she had
been consigned, was in her immediate neighborhood,
and that she might sometimes hear from her beloved
—at least till the Arctic ice separated them.

The following brief extract is made from her jour-
nal :—

"On the morning of the twenty-seventh of May,
1853.—After a tedious drive of four hours, I arrived
at Crookville—a manufacturing village situated on
Ridley Creek, and distant about eighteen miles from
Philadelphia. After various inquiries I reached the
house which was to be my home until Dr. Kane's
return to this country. With me first impressions
have much weight, and in a measure determine my
future feelings in regard either to houses or their inhabitants. Accordingly, I looked anxiously at the
pretty and unpretending dwelling which my beloved
had selected as my abode, and mentally I wondered
whether its inhabitants were as tasteful and neat as
their little home appeared to be. A few words will
suffice to describe this peaceful spot. The house is
surrounded by a picket fence, enclosing about an acre

of ground, which is very tastefully laid out in front with flower-beds containing many rare and beautiful specimens. Handsome trees offer an agreeable shade, while a pretty piazza covered with honeysuckles and roses forms a most inviting entrance."

On returning to New York Dr. Kane wrote :—

[Dr. Kane to Miss Fox.]

"MY OWN DEAR DARLING :—I arrived here this morning very tired, but with thoughts which excluded fatigue. Mrs. Walters I will see this afternoon, and send on the bird and other forgotten treasures by the early boat. They will be in Chester, care of *Sam Smith*, by Tuesday afternoon.

"On the same day, dear Maggie, my little bark will be ploughing the trackless sea. Will it be followed by your thoughts and prayers?

"When I think of our parting evening—its last hour, its last minutes—I am oppressed with the unreal vagueness of a dream. Oh, my Maggie, think of me—always think of me—with respect! Cling to me—always cling to me—with love! Lean on me, hope *in* me, bear with me—*trust me!* Let us remember the passing moments which time itself cannot destroy; moments sacred to affection, confidence, and love.

"And now, dear Maggie, my own dear Maggie, live a life of purity and goodness. Consecrate it to me. Wear no garb upon which even the breath of an angel could leave a stain. Thus live, dear Maggie, until God brings me back to you; and then, meeting my eye with the proud consciousness of virtue, we will resign ourselves to a passion sanctified by love and marriage. Golden fields shall spread before us their summer harvest—silver lakes mirror your very breath. Let us live for each other.

"Farewell.

"E. K. KANE."

"P. S. Write up to the last moment; they will tell you when we leave, at eleven A. M., Tuesday. Don't forget letters regularly.

"K."

On the return of Mrs. Fox from Philadelphia to New York on the twenty-seventh day of May, she was called on by Dr. Kane, who learned from her how distressed his poor Maggie had been, and in how disconsolate a condition she remained at school. He could not bear this; but, short as his time was, resolved on another journey to Crookville to snatch a few moments and have a last parting with one so deeply loved. He took with him the little bird referred to, which was named after him; but unfortunately lost it in Philadelphia. It was recovered, however, on his return, as related in the next missive.

[Dr. Kane to Miss Fox.]

" MY DEAR MAGGIE :—Upon my return to Philadelphia I offered a reward, and succeeded in obtaining our little bird. Thus, dear Maggie, you see that every thought, every wish, is met by me. Never doubt my love.

"Guard and cherish the little wanderer thus returned to the fold. Make it an evidence of my thoughtful attention to your every wish. An emblem, too, dear darling, of my own return, when, after a dreary flight, I come back to nestle in your bosom.

"Dispel all doubt, dear Maggie. Never reprove—never think unkindly. The day will come—bright as sunshine on the waters—when I claim your hand, and unrestrained by the trammels of our mutual dread, live with you in peace, tranquillity, and affection.

"Be good and pure. Restrain every thought

which interferes with a guileless life, and live to
prove by your improvement your love for

" Ly."

A sad parting, in truth, was this; though full of
youthful hope. Mrs. Turner could not fail to see
how deep and sincere was the Doctor's love for her
young charge.

7 *

XIV.

It will be remembered that Dr. Kane sailed on the
30th May, 1853, from New York. It is not necessary
to follow his progress northward; "this round un-
varnished tale" having reference only to his "course
of love." The uncertainty that hung over his return
was severely felt by her whom he found it hardest to
leave of all on earth. She treasured all the newspaper articles she could find. One of these dolefully
said:—"The experience of all Polar travellers seems
to show that after the first winter in that region, the
adventurer's effective energies are so subdued as to
render him practically worthless. Dr. Kane, therefore, though untrammelled by instructions, is strongly
advised to return in eighteen months. And should
two winters pass over the party ere we hail their return to receive the reward which is their due, our
people will not fall into the English error of waiting
four years in doubt as to their condition—but will
send at once a party to determine their fate."

Not long afterwards Margaret received a letter—as
follows—from the friend to whom Dr. Kane had
entrusted her matters.

[Mr. Grinnell to Miss Fox.]

"DEAR MISS·FOX:—I have received your two
letters; the latter informing me that you had not yet
received your trunks—which quite surprises me. I
have this morning written to your mother concerning
them, and if I can find time, I will go to see her this
evening. I am sorry to hear that you have lost your
little bird. I will send you another in the Doctor's name.
You will have seen by the papers which I sent to
you (and which you doubtless received), how well the
expedition went off. The day was beautiful, and
every man was in town at the appointed hour. As
the vessel passed along the wharves of the North
River, she was saluted with cheers from the crowds
assembled, and by guns from the shipping. Two
steamers accompanied us to sea, filled with people
The Doctor was in good spirits, and was quite well,
having entirely recovered from his rheumatic attack.

"They intend to touch at St. John's, Newfoundland,
for fresh meats,—whence we may expect to hear from
them in about a fortnight.

"I will send the bird the first opportunity, and
should any letters arrive, they shall be forwarded.

　　　　　　　"I am very truly yours,
　　　　　　　　　"C. GRINNELL."

Mr. Grinnell wrote—June 21st, 1853:

"You will be pleased to hear that 'The Advance' was spoken with on the 6th inst. off Sable Island, about half way to Newfoundland. She was going off at a fine rate, and the Doctor reported 'all well.' We may look for a letter from him in the course of this week.

"The weather to-day is excessively hot; the thermometer in the shade standing at 90.° I hope you received your trunks. I wrote to your mother concerning them."

———

The expected letter from Dr. Kane duly arrived, and the following was forwarded to Crookville by Mr. Grinnell. Some reference is made therein to recent censures passed about Margaret's abandonment of spiritualism, and her isolation from her family and friends for a lover's sake. The poor girl was extremely sensitive to gossip of this kind.

———

[Dr. Kane to Miss Fox]

"Just standing out to sea.

"Maggie, my own sweet pet, be comforted. I know you to be always good and pure, and I would sooner die than allow a breath of suspicion to tarnish your fair fame. Your letter gave me pain—pain because it showed me that you were unhappy. Oh, my Maggie, be not sad; accuse not me of unkindness; talk not thus of your Italian dream. You shall be to me as a cherished sister.

"To-day came your Sunday's letter—dear comforter to my wounded heart! Thank you, dear *Petie!* Thank you! Never shall you have cause to repent of me; never shall you say that I was not worthy of your trust and love.

"Do be comforted, my own angel—life of my soul —joy of my sad trials! Grieve not! Live the life of pure happiness for which you were destined. Regard me as a brother——anything but as one to be accused and mourned for.

"Grinnell will watch over you. Answer his letters. In a week you will hear from me again. Write to me within the next three days a long, long letter. It will reach me at Newfoundland. Do not grieve, but *trust*

"E. K. KANE.

"Have a care of my letters, darling."

Miss MARGARET FOX, Chester, Pa.

At Mr. Turner's, Crookville.

In the next letter Dr. Kane perhaps refers to the same complaining letter from the lonely girl he had separated from all her friends, and to the livelier missive that followed it.

[Dr. Kane to Miss Fox.]

"AT SEA, June 13th, 1853.

"DEAR DARLING MAGGIE :—Your one cruel letter was so beautifully erased by the kind one which followed it, that any unhappiness which it might have caused vanished like morning mists before the sunshine. One thing, however, pained me. The letter showed me that you were unhappy.

*   *   *   *   *   *

"For six months have I faltered in proofs of pure regard and love? Have you ever expressed before me an ungratified wish? Have I ever said a word uncalculated to elevate you? ever spoken of you to others but in terms such as a brother might speak of a sister? In everything I made you my *equal*.

*   *   *   *   *   *

"Live and bloom in purity as a flower kissed only by the morning dew. One thing you can never doubt: it is the truth of him who writes. Let it

then be as the bright sun upon the dewdrop, drinking up its waters into high heaven, and leaving the
flower unsullied by a caress. Be happy and true.
Strive to live that life which is its own reward;—
make the well-spent moments pave the future with
blessings;—and if ever on the eve of wrong, let this
be your guard: "Would dear 'Lish like me to do
this?"

———

[Dr. Kane to Miss Fox.]

* * "Now, dear *Petie*, let us talk of pleasanter
things. I think I see you in that quiet old country-
house—counting time by the village clock which
rises above the willows. Or, better still, I think I
see you under the shade of some drooping chestnut,
startling the birds—your playfellows—with dreamy
tokens from the spirit-world. There imagine me by
your side, and I'll answer all your questions.

"First,—about the 'German.' Study German by
all means. You say truly that it is a noble language
with a glorious literature; but apart from all this, *I*
know nothing of German, and I want you to be
ahead of me in something better than good looks and
spirit-trances.

"You can scold me in German, flirt with country
bumpkins in German, write naughty letters to me in

German, and I'll be none the wiser. Study the language by all means.

"Now for advice. Don't be afraid:—advice as to school matters.

"If you ask me to name the first branch in importance, let it be a good English foundation. Your own language, and the history and literature of the two great countries speaking it. Next, music; especially that voice of yours; and lastly, languages not so near home.

"Exercise at least three hours a day in the open air—wet or dry, rain or shine. Don't spare me with the shoemaking fraternity. Fun I regard as an essential element. Don't mope like a sickly cat. Why, Mag, I don't want to make a school-girl puppet—a strait-laced artificial automaton of you;—a mere hand-organ to grind out languages, and music, and long words! My only positive injunction to you is to exercise often, laugh when you can, grow as fat as you please; and when I return—God granting me that distant blessing—when I return, bowed down with the Polar frosts, let me have at least the rewarding consciousness of having done my duty.

"One thing more: should any trouble come to you —anything unforeseen, make —— your adviser and friend. I need not speak his name. Call upon him as one having my confidence, and therefore deserving yours.

"If at the end of four months you wish to try

another school-girl life, you are untrammelled. Do entirely as you please. North Carolina or Albany is before you; and if the former, which I should prefer, write to Dr. Hawks stating your intention, and Mr. ———— will give you funds; so that Mr. Turner can escort you. One final wish—the only thing like restraint that your true friend can find it in his heart to utter: See little of * * *, and *never sleep within her house.*

"God bless you!
"E. K. KANE.

"You see that I trust you."

———

Mr. Grinnell wrote:

"July 9th, 1853.

"DEAR MISS FOX:—I am about leaving town, and have only time to acknowledge the receipt of your note of the 5th inst., and trust that ere this you have received the letter forwarded to you a few days since from Dr. Kane. He sailed from St. John's on the 17th ult. for Greenland.

"I am,
"Very truly yours,
"C. GRINNELL."

On the 10th August, 1853, Mr. Grinnell wrote from the yacht " Albion " in the harbor of Newport, R. I.:

" We have heard nothing from Dr. Kane since I forwarded his last letter to you. We shall probably hear from him again in October from Greenland by Capt. Inglefield in the Phœnix, or perhaps by the whalers."

———

On the 23d of the same month, he writes, in relation to a proposed change in Margaret's school which would bring her nearer her New York friends:

" As regards your leaving Mrs. Turner's for Mrs. Willard's of Troy, if my advice were asked, I should say decidedly—remain where you are at present; since you find Mrs. Turner's so comfortable and pleasant in all respects, whereas at Mrs. Willard's you might not enjoy yourself so much. And as far as your education is concerned, it appears to me that nothing could be better than the course you are now pursuing at Mrs. Turner's. I am desirous, however, of following the wishes of Dr. Kane, and would take the liberty of advising you to think well of the matter before you decide to make a change. We cannot expect to receive letters from the Doctor until September or October "

Again, a few days after—approving Margaret's determination to remain at Crookville—he says :

" We shall probably hear from Dr. Kane by the end of next month "

———

The deference to her wish to hear continually from the absent one thus shown to Margaret by Dr. Kane's most trusted friend, evinces his knowledge of the engagement existing between them.   To Mr. Grinnell Dr. Kane had entrusted the funds to be forwarded to Miss Fox from time to time, to meet the expenses of her school bills.

Dr. Kane's aunt, Mrs. Leiper, occasionally saw Miss Fox, enquired concerning her progress in her studies, and seemed much interested therein.   Once at her own house, she made the young lady play for her, to see how she was getting on with her music.

The sorrow of the poor girl so affected her health that it was thought prudent to permit her to take a short vacation to visit her friends in New York. Dr. Bayard, a distinguished physician, advised it ; and Mrs. Walter, a sister of the Hon. John Cochrane, and connected by marriage with Bishop Potter's family, came to Crookville for her, and brought Margaret to spend some days at Mrs. W——'s house in Clinton Place. Here she suffered from a severe illness brought on by mental disquiet. The following letter is from her friend Mrs. Turner, the mother of her governess.

———

November 6th, 1853.

" Little—my dear child—did I dream that you were tossing on a fevered bed, or I would have written to you before this. It is very sad to think that you went for so brief a space to enjoy the society of your friends, and were stricken down with such a malady. But if we could but bring our rebellious hearts to think so at the time, every event which happens to us is for the best. Had you been taken ill here, you know how difficult it would have been to obtain *good* medical advice ; now you are among friends and relations, and have the advice of your own physician, which will go a great way in effecting a cure. Therefore cheer up. You have youth on your side ; but when you are able to rise, you must be very careful for fear of a relapse ; and when you are quite convalescent, you will have to work harder than ever, to make up for lost time.

" I am glad to see by the papers that there have been satisfactory accounts of our mutual and far distant friend. When you are able, I will expect a *long* letter from you. In the mean time,

"I remain your affectionate friend,

"S. TURNER."

The same lady, uneasy at the prolonged absence of her pupil, thus wrote:

[Mrs. Turner to Miss Fox.]

"CROOKVILLE, Dec. 12th, 1853.

"MY DEAR MARGARET:—Not having received any communication from you since I wrote to you last, I am feeling many anxieties on your account. If you were laid on a bed of sickness, surely you would get some friend to write a few lines to me mentioning your situation. If, on the other hand, your health is quite re-established, and you are merely remaining to indulge in the gaieties of the city, you should write to me yourself. You know I am always willing to make every reasonable allowance for young people; but my indulgence has a limit. *   *   *

" And now, dear Margaret, I come to a part of the subject about which I feel very much concerned. On the last interview which I had with Dr. Kane, I promised to be like a mother to you while under my charge; to cultivate your understanding, and enable you to call forth those latent energies which lay dormant through neglect; and, above all, to guard you from influences which might prove hostile to your progress in the attainment of those virtues and accomplishments which are indispensable to the female character. I endeavored to fulfil my promise, and your progress was in some respects highly satisfactory to me. But how shall I account to that noble-minded friend for this cessation from well-doing—or, to use a harsher term, this lapse from duty! Ask your own heart if it be right."

———

Mrs. W—— thus replied to Mrs. Turner's letter:

[Mrs. W—— to Mrs. Turner.]

"MY DEAR MRS. TURNER:—Maggie is very much distressed by the contents of your last letter; although it may seem, from her not having informed you fully of the reasons for her remaining here so long, that you had just cause for censure.

"I am happy to disabuse your mind. She has been far from well, and under the medical care of Dr. Edward Bayard—brother of the Hon. James Bayard, late Minister to Brussels—who has thought it important for her to remain; indeed, it is only within the last few days that she has looked at all like herself. Neither has she partaken of the amusements and gaieties of the city, not having inclination nor the strength for them. Her associations have been of the most refined character, such as I know Dr. Kane and yourself would most highly approve of; and although her absence from her studies is to be regretted, I trust her time has not been altogether misemployed. We were all delighted with Maggie's improvement, showing the great care and tenderness bestowed upon her. Your letter only proves what a sincere friend you are to her.

"You will rejoice to hear that your fears are groundless. Could you have witnessed the distress mingled with the strong affection she feels for you, on reading your letter, you would have loved her more than ever, as I confess I did. Some of the elements of Maggie's character are very beautiful, and with the cultivation she has been receiving while under your care, will make her all that her best friends wish her to be. She will leave here two weeks from to-morrow; and if anything unforeseen should occur in the mean time, to change the day, she will inform you. Hoping that this will relieve your mind concerning Maggie, believe me, with great respect,

"Yours truly,
Ellen W——."

"I would add, the reason why Maggie has not written, has been the hope that she would be well enough to leave from week to week, but the protracted character of her indisposition has prevented. The Doctor, whom I have just seen, thinks that in a fortnight her health will be firmly established, so that she may pursue her studies with advantage.

" E. W."

————

" CROOKVILLE, Dec. 15th, 1853.

" MY DEAR MRS. W——:—I have just received your highly welcome favor of the 14th inst; it has truly been to me a messenger of peace, for it has relieved my mind from those keen anxieties which I could not help feeling on account of my young friend. Had she but written me a few lines it would have saved me many a sleepless hour.

" I regret exceedingly that I should have said one word calculated to wound her feelings, and hope she will attribute the hasty expression of my thoughts to the true cause, anxiety for her ultimate welfare. Had I been aware of the protracted nature of her indisposition I would have felt glad that she was with kind old friends, and near competent medical advisers. Being unaware of the real state of the case, and receiving no answers to my letters, I really began to fear that she had fallen under those influences from which it has been the aim and object of kind friends to shield her. She must not think the worse of me for performing my duty to her, though it should occasionally be a hard one.

* * * * * *

"I feel much gratified to hear that you are pleased with her progress, and think that she has made some improvement. She was very industrious, and never lost a moment. But she suffered so much from toothache as well as other bodily infirmities, that sometimes it was difficult to accomplish much. I hope Margaret will not think of undertaking the journey till she is fully able to travel.

"Please present my kindest love to her, in which Mr. Turner heartily joins.

"And believe me yours truly,

"S. TURNER."

[Mrs. Turner to Miss Fox.]

"CROOKVILLE, Dec. 29th, 1853.

"MY DEAR MARGARET:—I dispatched a few lines to you this morning, but in the course of the day I received a letter from Mr. Grinnell, wishing to know at what time you returned to Crookville! I have just written to him, stating that Mrs. W—— had written to me that you had been unable to resume

8

your studies till your health should be re-established.
But he will most probably wait on you himself.

"Hoping soon to see you,

"I remain yours sincerely,

"S. TURNER."

———

Mrs. W—— wrote to Margaret at school, March
7th, 1854—as follows:

"I was delighted, dear Maggie, to receive your
note. The letters all came safely. I thought yours
to the Doctor very sweet and touching from their
sympathy and the pure affection breathing throughout
them. What is more to be prized than a pure, devoted heart? I will take the best care of them, and
send them, as you directed, to Mr. Grinnell.

"We had a delightful visit with you in your plea
sant home. I was so much pleased with Mrs. Turner
and her family. Mr. Turner I liked very much.
You are favored, dear Maggie, in the seclusion of
your residence; but one of these days you will come
out of it, and shine all the brighter. Then you will
feel and know the great advantage of an education,
and will fully appreciate the noble friend who gave
it, and to whom you have given your heart's best
love.

" Good night, dear, sweet little Maggie, and may sweet spirits hover ever near you.

" Yours ever,

" ELLEN W——."

———

Another letter dated March 15th, 1854, is from Mr. Grinnell.

" MY DEAR MISS FOX :—I have received your note of yesterday, and take the earliest opportunity to inform you that Dr. Kane by no means considers the search for Sir John Franklin as useless; on the contrary, *he is full of hope*, and left here under the full conviction that the missing party were still in existence. I shall feel much obliged if you will please send me the article you refer to in the Cincinnati paper, as such an erroneous statement should be contradicted.

" Captain Inglefield, of the steamer Phœnix, will leave England in April for the Arctic regions. Should you wish to write to Dr. Kane by this conveyance, please send your letter to me before next Saturday, as the steamer Baltic leaves on that day for England. You should therefore put your letter in the post-office (addressed to me) Thursday afternoon, if possible, or early Friday morning.

"I am very truly yours,
"C. GRINNELL.

"By express I send you Dr. Kane's book."

In a note dated March 30th, he wrote: "I have not received any letter from you to be forwarded to Dr. Kane. I fear it is now too late."

" April 7th, 1854.—We do not expect to hear from Dr. Kane until next September or October."

He wrote—

" April 21st, 1854.

" MY DEAR MISS FOX :—I have received your note of the 20th, and in compliance with your request I have written to Mrs. Turner (letter enclosed) to request permission for you to visit your friends in this city, and she will doubtless accede to your wishes."

" July 17th, 1854.

"My Dear Miss Fox :—I enclose a letter for you just received from the Doctor. It should have been here some time ago ; but you know that the mails are not very regular from that distant quarter of the globe.

"Please inform me if you are in need of money, and I will immediately forward whatever amount you may require.

" I sincerely trust that we may again see our good friend the Doctor back again in October, and that he may be successful in his noble undertaking.

" I am very truly yours,
"Cornelius Grinnell."

The above reached Crookville during Margaret's temporary absence, and Mrs. Turner wrote :

" Crookville, July 29th, 1854.

" My Dear Margaret :—I write to acquaint you that a letter from Mr. Grinnell, enclosing one from

Dr. Kane, arrived here to-day. On leaving this, you requested Lizzy to open any letter which might come from Mr. Grinnell during your absence. I accordingly opened this; but on finding the enclosure, I immediately folded both in the envelope, *unread.* Now, Margaret, I am really at a loss to know what to do with this. Several of our letters and papers have gone astray lately from the negligence of the post-office officials. And, judging how very dear and precious this letter must be to you, I feel very unwilling to run any risk of its going astray in transmitting it to you by post. I therefore think you had better come for it yourself; or write me word immediately on receipt of this, whether I shall return it to Mr. Grinnell or not.

"I remain your perplexed friend,

" S. TURNER."

XV

The above, as may be supposed, brought the truant young lady back to school forthwith. Here is Dr. Kane's letter, portions of which must be omitted on account of observations on persons which would not be understood by the reader.

————

[Dr. Kane to Miss Fox.]

"DEAR, DEAR MAGGIE :—In the midst of ice and desolation I still think of you. Can you, while hope and sunshine linger round you, turn a thought to me ?

"Only a few minutes, dear Maggie, have I to renew my assurances of confidence and trust. You cannot but love and honor your only and truest friend. Be then all that I have advised you to be, and thus reward me for an act which the harsh world could neither understand nor appreciate.

*　　*　　*　　*　　*　　*

"Trust in my honor, dear Maggie, and you and your 'treasured secrets' will always be as in your

own heart alone. For am not *I* your heart? Yes,
dear Mag, your very heart of hearts—now and always!
                                                    "Ly.

"P. S.—Your portrait is a great comfort to me. I
often gaze on its quiet loveliness."

In a letter written to his father, and probably sent
with the above, Dr. Kane had this postscript: "Love.
☞ My last word is 'Love.' " It may well be con-
jectured to whom he referred.

Mr. Grinnell wrote :—

"I trust you have received the letter I sent to you
a few days since from the Doctor, from Greenland.

"He deserves success in his noble and daring enterprise, and I am sure he will achieve it. The nation
may well feel proud of him. I will write to you in
the early part of the week, and I remain
                    "Very truly yours,
                                    "C. Grinnell."

He wrote while Miss Fox was still in New York:—

—— "The last mail brings accounts of the return

of Captain Inglefield, and I have no doubt that by the
mail to arrive here on Friday or Saturday, we shall
have letters from Dr. Kane.

"Where and when shall I send the money?"

————

August 17th, 1854, Mr. Grinnell wrote:—

"We may look for the Doctor about the 10th of
October. Trusting that his life and health have been
spared, and that he may have been successful in finding some trace of the lost ones—

"I am, etc."

————

Still later, he announces that "Captain Inglefield
has returned, but brings no news of Dr. Kane."

Again:—

"We may hear from Dr. Kane by the steamer to
arrive from England next week. Should any letters
come for you, I will forward them without delay."

————

October 17th, 1854 :—

" We have no tidings yet of the Doctor; nor do
we look for him until the latter end of the month.
My father says that if he is not at home by the end
of November, that he will conclude that he intends
to remain another winter in the Arctic regions.

"I shall certainly inform you if we receive any
tidings from the Doctor.

"You will perceive by the papers that Sir Edward
Belcher has abandoned his squadron, and has returned to England, leaving Dr. Kane alone in the
field."

————

The "hope deferred" that makes the heart sick
was to be experienced by the friends of the adventurous explorer for many weary months. And who
felt more painfully his prolonged absence—that dreary
interval when no tidings came, and gloom rested on
the future—than she, the chosen of his heart, whose
every hope of the future was interwoven with thoughts
of him! What had she on earth to look forward to
but the meeting with her lover and friend—long-lost,
and dearer than ever! Her connection with spiritualism was for ever severed; its votaries were no longer
her friends; she no longer looked to it for her sup-

port. Her life was bound up in that of the absent one.

———

The following letter is from Miss Gray, the daughter of a physician in New York. She was a lovely and accomplished girl, and an intimate friend of Margaret's.

"October 12th, 1854.

"I received your little note yesterday, Maggie Pet, and duly delivered the note for Kate into her own hands. She said she would answer it immediately. And now, old lady, I have a bone to pick with you. I shall not write to you again until you find out what my name is, and call me by it. I love you *too* much, *dear one*, to address you as 'Miss Fox;' then why will you do it towards me? I always fancied you cared a little bit about poor me, but when your letters come with 'My dear Miss Gray' at the commencement, I fairly give up all hope. Write whenever you can, sweet Maggie; I am always willing and most happy to do anything in my power for you, and therefore hope if there is anything that I can do for you in any way, you will write and tell me.

"And now adieu! Uncle sends his best regards, father and mother their love, and I my very *best* love.

And with the hope of soon seeing you, allow me to remain as ever

"Your friend,

"GERALDINE GRAY.

"P. S.—I saw in a paper of last week that the Doctor would probably be absent longer than he anticipated when he left. But, dear Maggie, if he is only spared to return to you after his perilous journey, that is all you can ask. I pray that he may be guarded safely.

"Ever your friend,

"GERALDINE."

[Miss Gray to Miss Fox.]

"NEW YORK, Oct. 31st.

"MY DEAR MAGGIE:—I have been for the past two weeks staying at Newburgh, and thence accompanied my friends (Hon. H. Ramsdell's family) to Niagara, where we stayed a week; and having just returned, find a most welcome letter from you, dated the twelfth of this month. I hasten to reply, to erase from your mind the impression of its not being received.

"I am heartily glad, Maggie pet, you have found out my Christian name; for I have had a good many heart-twinges in reference to your apparent coldness.

"I suppose, of course, Maggie, the Doctor will soon return, now that his efforts are no more needed. How *very* glad I am for your sake! Oh, may your lot in life be blessed and happy! calm and cloudless to the end!

"If the reports are all correct, you have now a treasure—one that will guard you with an ever kind and jealous watchfulness; jealous, I said! Yes! for who will not guard those they hold dearest and nearest, with jealous care! Maggie, darling, accept my prayers and well wishes for your future. Do not deem me forward, dearest; for I love you too dearly not to feel a deep, deep interest in those things which will add one iota to your worldly happiness.

"I have not as yet seen either your mother or Katie; when I do, I shall punctually deliver your message about 'Tommy.'

"And now, Maggie, for fear of tiring your kindness and patience, I will e'en draw my stupid letter to a close, hoping *soon* to hear from you. Your letters are ever acceptable and welcome; so deem it not lost time when you spare a few moments to remember one who may most truly sign herself one of

"Your most affectionate friends,

"GERALDINE GRAY."

"CROOKVILLE, Dec. 7th, 1854.

"MY DEAR MRS. W——:—I have just received yours of the 6th inst., and feel perfectly satisfied with your explanation of the cause of my young friend's protracted stay in New York. I did not by any means censure Margaret for leaving this at the time she did; for I really pitied her from my inmost heart, and felt that she required change of scene to dissipate the sickness of the heart which arises from hope deferred. Had she told me on parting that she wished to remain a month with you, I would not have made the slightest objection; but I have ever impressed on young persons the folly of making rash promises, and the sacred duty of keeping a promise when once made, no matter at what cost.

"I have always found Margaret much improved in many respects from her visits to you; more cheerful in her mind, and more punctual in her habits," etc.

———

Mr. Grinnell wrote :

"APRIL 30th, 1855.

"If the Doctor returns this year, he will probably be here in October next; but if he is not home by that time, he cannot get here before October, 1856.

"The Government Expedition in search of him and his party will leave here on the 1st of June, and they are expected to return in October following."

———

Each of the numerous letters of this gentleman shows that he recognised in Miss Fox the betrothed wife of his friend—as such respecting her anxiety to hear the earliest news. The letters of Mrs. Turner show the tender affection with which the young lady was regarded by her instructress. That excellent friend found it necessary to resume the tone of reproof—

[Mrs. Turner to Miss Fox.]

"JULY 3d, 1855.

"I trust in a kind Providence that Dr. Kane will return in the course of this ensuing fall, to greet his friends and country. He will expect to find your mind stored with the elements of useful knowledge. He will expect to find a companion whose conversational powers have been cultivated. Ask yourself, my dear child, one question, without flinching from the task: 'How shall I meet those requirements? How have I improved those precious talents committed to my charge? Have there been no wasted days, or weeks? no slighted opportunities, or neglected means?' If the echo of your inmost heart responds a 'no' to your searching appeal, then shall your 'bosom's lord sit lightly on its throne!'

"It is my earnest hope and prayer that you will improve every hour * * . I do not in the least fear your forgetting 'The Pleasures of Hope'—but the recorded events of the past cannot be remembered without exertion and severe study. I need say nothing about your music, except that your daily practising should be in earnest. Do not think me too hard in thus speaking to you as I would to my own daughters. Did I do otherwise, I should ill perform the trust reposed in me by one now far, far distant."

———

She writes—July 16th, 1855:—"As your return to New York will not take place till the middle or last of September, the probability is that Dr. Kane will have arrived by that time. I feel really sorry that you should have been called away just at the time when every moment was doubly precious."

———

[Mrs. Turner to Miss Fox.]

" CROOKVILLE, July 20th, 1855.

"MY DEAR MARGARET:—I have just received your little note, mailed on Saturday. I also received one from Mr. Grinnell by same post. He says you will be here by first of August, to commence again in right good earnest. So you must make up your mind to have hard study all this fall. I wrote you my reasons for not being able to fulfil my promise of going to New York to conduct you here. You will therefore have to provide some other escort. If you had a friend to accompany you as far as Philadelphia, and put you on board the Media cars, Market and Elizabeth streets, we would await you at Wallingford station, at six P. M. At all events write me word what way you will come, that I may meet you. I hope you will not leave any of your things behind; and be sure and bring a supply of music. Some pretty new songs, which you can learn without much difficulty. You have quite forgotten to date any of the notes I have received from you. Never write anything, however unimportant, without a date."

The reader must not suppose, from the complaints of her anxious friend, that Margaret ever undervalued

the advantages she enjoyed at Crookville, or weakly
yielded to her own inclinations for the society of her
kindred—enfeebled as she was in health. She was
urged to prolong her vacations, by those friends in whom
both she and Mrs. Turner had perfect confidence.
One of these was suffering severely in health, and it
was in Maggie's power to soothe and alleviate those
sufferings. Thus, her stay in New York was often
urged as a matter of *duty*, to which she ought to sacrifice her own interests. She had nothing to do with
spiritualism; her hatred to that, and her aversion to
its votaries, increased every day.

The annexed letter from Mrs. Bayard was sent to
Margaret while at school.

New York, Sept. 3d.

"My Dear Maggie :—I delayed replying to your
letter, thinking that, as Mrs. Kemyes wrote you last
week, you would be glad to hear still later how we
were getting on. I am most happy to say that my
dear husband is still free from pain, and is most
sanguine that he will reach the 27th without any
severe spasm. I trust in this he may not be disappointed. We have not heard a word from Katie
since she left. Is she not a naughty girl not to keep

her promise! We all want to hear from her very
much. Mrs. Kemyes received a letter from Mrs.
——, this morning, who is pretty well, and enjoying
her visit very much. She will probably remain at
Petersboro' a week or two longer. I think the Dr.
and myself will leave town in a day or two, to be
absent some time—but how long I cannot say; I hope
two weeks; but where we shall go we have not yet
decided. The country air will do the Dr. great good,
as will also the rest from his professional labors. I
long to get away from the din and dust of this great
town, and 'repose' for a while in some quiet spot.
Do you not enjoy this charming autumnal weather?
It is just the weather for study, and I am sure you
are deeply engaged, and are making rapid progress,
so that when your long absent one returns, he will
have great pleasure in finding you all he could
desire.

"We were glad to hear that you were so well,
and now you must keep so; for I want you to greet
the stranger with a sweet blooming face; such a one
as he has not seen during his two years' absence, only
in his dreams! It is now raining very fast, and
everything looks dreary. I wish you were here to
cheer me up a little.

"Bye bye, with much love and sincere wishes for
your health and happiness.

"Truly yours,
"T. BAYARD.

"N. B. The Dr. sends much love, and says that he is quite impatient for the 29th to arrive, so that he may see you."

———

The appointment for "the 29th" was to meet Dr. Bayard and Mrs. ——— in Philadelphia. The party went thence to Harrisburgh to visit Mr. Henry Bayard. After returning to school for a few days, Margaret was taken to New York by Mrs. K——, when the following letter came:

[Mrs. Turner to Miss Fox.]

Crookville, Oct. 12th, 1855.

"MY DEAR MARGARET:—As you may suppose, I was much disappointed, on my return from the city, to find you absent. Expecting every day either to hear from you or see you, I deferred writing till to-day. At dinner-time Mr. Turner announced the glad tidings of Dr. Kane's arrival. I was too much overjoyed to eat, and now sit down to offer you my hearty congratulations on his safe arrival. Though he may not have accomplished all he anticipated, his return will be hailed with delight by his admiring country; and the exertions he has so bravely made in the cause of nautical discovery be generously rewarded.

"And now, dear Margaret, as it is not at all probable that you and I shall resume our pleasant studies
together, I hope the remembrance of those hours we
have spent in conversation or reading, will long continue to afford you happy thoughts. You will have
to consult with your friends about the best means of
having your trunks sent from this, and when you
have decided, send me word. Surely you will come
and see me—that we may have one good long talk
more, together. Present my kindest regards to Mrs.
W——, and by all means kind *love* to the Doctor.
In this Mr. Turner and the girls join. Let me hear
from you by return of mail, and believe me

"Yours affectionately,
"Susannah Turner."

XVI.

The foregoing extracts from the letters of persons esteemed and trusted by Dr. Kane—one of them his most intimate friend—may serve to show not only the respect and affection with which they regarded Margaret Fox, but their recognition of the tender relation subsisting between her and the navigator. They all regarded her as the affianced wife of Dr. Kane, and expected the marriage to take place soon after his return to America. Known as this engagement was to many, it was not surprising that the rumor was spread abroad, and that newspaper announcements of the adventurous explorer being about to return, or having arrived, should be mingled with mention of his approaching nuptials. A newspaper statement, that "the celebrated Dr. Kane would shortly lead to the altar Miss Margaret Fox, of spirit-rapping celebrity," went the rounds of the press in every quarter of the country; and other manufacturers of news were busy in arranging the particulars. Only a few of these articles met the eye of the lady most interested; but they came from far and near to the relatives of Dr. Kane, and their pride was deeply wounded.

It had been undoubtedly the expectation of Dr.

Kane himself, hoping to find the education of his beloved one completed, to marry her as soon as his circumstances permitted. He had directed that at the wedding she should wear the singular ornament of a carbuncle upon her forehead, which he was to procure for her. Margaret had arranged with her friend, Mrs. ——, that the ceremony should take place at her house, in the presence of a select circle of friends. The dresses for the occasion had of course been discussed; for when did ladies talk of a wedding in prospect without mention of the dresses?

Margaret was absent from school on one of her visits to New York, and was staying with Mrs. W——, when the event so long anticipated, looked forward to with such trembling delight, took place. One morning in October a note was handed to the young lady. It announced the safe arrival of the Doctor. His ship was expected the very next day.

As the vessel came up the Bay of New York, Margaret heard the guns fired in joyful greeting. Her excitement became so great that her careful friend would not permit her to stir out, but insisted on her remaining as quiet as possible. All that evening, when it was known that Dr. Kane was in the city, they waited for the ring of the bell that should herald his visit. Till midnight they listened every moment for his familiar step. He did not come. The next morning it was the same. They waited expectant till noon. The young lady's feelings may be imagined.

At length the friends concluded that the strange delay
was caused by the Doctor's not knowing that his
"Maggie" was in New York. Mr. Grinnell knew
nothing of this last visit; how could his friend be
expected to know it? He might even then be setting
out for Crookville to see her. Mrs. W—— immediately wrote a note—her young friend was too much
agitated to pen it herself—and it was dispatched to
Mr. Grinnell to inform him Miss Fox was in Clinton
Place.

Little did those who offered their joyous congratulations to the wanderer who had returned covered with
glory to his native land, imagine the anguish of one
heart—shrouded from the jubilant public—yet beating
alone for him who had so often bidden her "trust his
honor." Wearied out with disappointed expectation,
and the distress of being compelled to doubt the truth
of her heart's idol, Margaret left Clinton Place that
night, and went to the house in Tenth street where
her mother and younger sister, Katharine, resided.
She was quite exhausted with what she had under-
gone during the day, and threw herself upon a
couch.

It was very late in the evening when she was suddenly startled by a hasty ringing at the door bell.
Then a friend's voice was heard, calling her, as he
came up stairs. He brought the news that a carriage
—no doubt containing Dr. Kane—had stopped at Mrs.
W——'s door in Clinton Place. Mrs. W——, on

seeing the carriage, had sent him in haste to bring her friend. "Make haste, my child, and come with me, for you must see him," he cried, and eagerly drew Margaret down stairs and out of the house. She had no time to collect her thoughts; but one idea was paramount, and overcame all the bitterness that had filled her heart. She was going to see him again!

Supported and almost carried along by her old friend and physician, who was with her, the poor girl reached Mrs. W——'s door; but was met by the lady with hardly coherent apologies. It was all a mistake, a gentleman on business, not Dr. Kane!

Mrs. W—— did not dare then to tell her young friend that the visitor in the carriage was Mr. Cornelius Grinnell, who came at Dr. Kane's request, to say he would come shortly; and to explain the circumstances that had prevented his coming immediately on his arrival.

There was "great trouble in his family" on account of his engagement; he had been beset on all sides by the remonstrances of relatives and friends; he was suffering severely from rheumatism; but so anxious to come that he would do so as soon as possible, etc. Such were the excuses made to Mrs. W——. She persuaded her friend to stay with her all night.

Another object Mr. Grinnell had in view, was, to procure the letters addressed by Dr. Kane to Miss Fox, which he supposed to be in Mrs. W——'s keeping. Had he seen the young lady herself, and pre-

9

ferred such a request to her, she would no doubt have
instantly placed them in his hands. Mrs. W——
said nothing to her on the subject, nor did she ever
know they had been asked for till years had elapsed
after Dr. Kane's death. She was and is assured, that
such a request came not from Dr. Kane, but from
some of his family.

About nine the next morning, Dr. Kane, wearing
his naval uniform, came, and was received by Mrs.
——. "Where is Maggie?" was his first question.
"She is above stairs—but the child is completely
broken down," was the reply. The Doctor asked to
see her, but Margaret's answer was a refusal to receive
him. Mrs. W—— went to intercede for her visitor,
who appeared to suffer scarcely less than she had
done. But woman's pride had come to the young
girl's aid, and she was firm in declining to see the
Doctor; adding, that it was her wish that the engagement between them should be broken off from that
moment and for ever.

Dr. Kane persisted in his entreaties for an interview, and Mrs. W—— begged for it on his behalf.
"For the love you bear me, Maggie," she pleaded,
with tears, "go down and see Dr. Kane." Her petition
prevailed; the young girl reluctantly consented, and
went down to the parlor. The Doctor was walking
the room in a fearful state of excitement. When he
saw her, he came near, clasped her firmly in his arms,
and kissed her head and her brow many times, hold-

ing her for some minutes closely pressed to his breast.
Both were in tears.

In broken words Dr. Kane expressed his joy at
meeting once more her whom he still loved so fondly
—who was to him "the same as when we parted."
He told her how he had been prevented from hastening to see her; how, that very morning, he had been
forced to tear himself away—to rush from the house
unprepared for a visit to a lady; "not half dressed,"
as he termed it. The conversation was long, and
Margaret listened patiently and kindly, though its
purport was to inform her that all idea of their marriage must be indefinitely postponed on account of
the violent opposition of Dr. Kane's family and relatives. For the present, they must be to each other
only as sister and brother!

The Doctor then drafted a note or statement, which
he said was to satisfy his mother. It was an acknow-
ledgement on Miss Fox's part that the relations
between them were merely friendly and fraternal;
that no matrimonial engagement had subsisted, etc.,
etc.

The poor girl's dream of love and happiness was
already over. But her heart was tender, and she had
no pride to forbid her pitying the distress endured by
one still so dear to her. She felt for his embarrass-
ment; she wished to restore peace between him and
his family; and without one selfish thought, she con-
tented to sign the statement.

She accordingly copied it in her own handwriting, the Doctor directing her as her trembling hand guided the pen. Her single remonstrance—"Doctor, this is not right—*it is not true*"—was silenced by his excuses; by pleadings that he was worried beyond endurance on all sides, and that the happiness of those he was bound to reverence and love depended on it. "Do it for me, Maggie!" he urged; "you shall never suffer! It is for my mother!"

He then called in Mrs. W——, to show her the statement. She looked surprised at her young friend, and said, "Maggie, is this so?"

The poor girl—weakened as she was by mental anguish, and hardly knowing what to do—could not withstand this direct appeal. "No—no—it is not so!" she sobbed. "Doctor Kane knows it is not! Remember what you said in the carriage—" referring to a particular conversation with Dr. Kane, in which their wedding preparations had been talked of in detail.

The Doctor appeared annoyed at this denial. "You are not the Maggie I took you for," he exclaimed.

But it was far from Margaret's intention to make any claim upon his honor for the continuance or fulfilment of their engagement. She freely consented to have it dissolved for ever; and if she yielded to his entreaties that she would still receive his visits as a brother, it was because she believed him the greatest sufferer, and was willing to do all in her power to soothe and comfort him.

In spite of Mrs. W——'s disapproval the written statement was given to the Doctor, who said he would take it to his mother.

It is due to him to relate that, a few days afterwards, he handed back the statement to Margaret, with the significant remark—"The wicked shall not inherit the kingdom of heaven." She tore it in pieces on the spot, without ever looking to see if it were in her own handwriting. Thus perished, she believed, the record of her only act of disingenuousness.

With all her deep affection for Dr. Kane—an affection now entwined with every fibre of her being—Margaret felt a relief in having matters thus settled on a basis which she was assured would be satisfactory to his friends. She loved him so purely and unselfishly, that her chief thought was for him—for his welfare and his happiness, in preference to her own. Dr. Kane always ingenuously acknowledged to her that he had been compelled by his persecutors to act a part unworthy of a gentleman.

He showed her a letter written to him by his aunt, Mrs. Leiper, who had seen some of the newspaper articles. She bade him clear himself of the imputation of having deceived that young girl—whom he had placed under her own charge—or *never enter her house again!* The Doctor said—"See, Maggie, here is my favorite aunt turning against me for your sake!"

One Sunday morning, when Miss Fox was just going to early mass, a carriage drove up, with Dr. Kane and a gentleman whom he introduced to Miss Fox as Mr. C—— Van R —— Taking Mrs. Fox aside, he told her the man had forced himself upon him, and was determined to enquire of her whether there were really any engagement existing between Margaret and the Doctor. He bade her tell him the engagement had been kindly broken off. This Van R—— was connected with a newspaper, and was a friend of some of the Doctor's acquaintances. Miss Maggie had heard evil reports of him, and asked Dr. Kane how he could associate with a man so notorious. He replied that he was no associate of his, and seemed mortified at being in his company.

Dr. Kane always evinced respect and regard for those who took part with Margaret, even though they censured his own conduct.

The friends of Miss Fox were not disposed to treat him with the same leniency she had shown. She herself sometimes expressed her wish that all intercourse might cease between them, since they were no longer on the same footing of affianced lovers. But the Doctor earnestly pleaded against such a decision. On the same morning that witnessed their first stormy interview he said, "I must see Maggie again this evening." He came in the evening to Clinton Place, and not finding her there, went immediately to Tenth Street. There he had a hurried conversation with

Margaret, whom he besought to stand firm, and to be
true to him, till the storm had blown over. He
would not be separated from her; his love was as
strong as ever; he would be firm as a rock, and he
entreated her still to confide in him.

Several brief letters were sent by Dr. Kane about
this time, from which an extract or two will suffice to
show his feelings.

————

[Dr. Kane to Miss Fox.]

" You do right, my own dear darling, and I will
aid and strengthen you in your good resolutions.
Lean upon me as on a brother, and receive my admiration and respect. I will call at seven o'clock this
afternoon—perhaps at six. Do be in.

" God bless you."

————

[Dr. Kane to Miss Fox.]

* * " Send me word, therefore, by the bearer, if
wish to see me, and at what hour. Let Katie write
the note, for you are not the Maggie which you used
to be. I have waited many days—but to-morrow I

must return. Be assured of one thing : that whatever you may do, or say, or think, not one word shall
ever come from me that can wound you. Even as
my sister, I will guard you; and whatever you may
do, will now, as always, be a gentleman.

"P.S.—I leave at nine to-morrow morning."

To Mrs. Fox, who strove to prevent his seeing her
daughter, Dr. Kane said many times that he was at
present dependent on his father for the means of
living; but that when his book should be published,
and he had time to receive the returns, he would be
his own master. Then he could afford to act inde-
pendently, and could spurn the interference of
friends who had already wrought so much mischief.

Amid all his sorrow one fear seemed to harass him
perpetually—that Miss Fox might be induced to
return to the professional life she had abandoned
years ago for his sake. She was surrounded by spi-
ritualists, and at that time was still in possession of
the mysterious power which she was doubtless often
entreated to exercise. This uneasiness is evident in
the following letter, which breathes the tone of former
times. It is proper to add that he was mistaken in
his fears, for which there existed no ground.

XVII.

[Dr. Kane to Miss Fox.]

"DEAR MAGGIE:—Do not be uneasy—I am sick, but the doctors make more of it than it deserves, in order to keep me abed.

"Your letter of Sunday reached me yesterday, but my chest gave me too much pain to write. I will see you, if I am well enough, on Wednesday afternoon at five o'clock. Do avoid 'spirits.' I cannot bear to think of you as engaged in a course of wickedness and deception. Indeed, Maggie, it is very sad. Say so to Kate.

"Take care of your cough, and excuse the low spirits of the 'Preacher.' God bless you. Bye bye.

"P. S.—Excuse my talking about the 'spirits.' You know that I never mention them on paper; but, Maggie, I'm really sick, and perhaps am cross. If anything was to happen to me, what would become of Kate and yourself? Maggie, you have no friend whose interest in you is disconnected from this cursed rapping. Pardon my saying so; but is it not deceit even *to listen when others are deceived?* Am I not a true friend to warn you against it? In childhood it may be a mere indiscretion; but what will it be when

9*

hard age wears its wrinkles into you, and like * *, you grow old!

"Dear Maggie, I could cry to think of it. No wonder that you are so nervous—that the doors shake and the windows tremble with the wind of night. A time will come when you will see the *real* ghost of memory—an awful spectre! * * * * Read this to dear Katie; both of you can depend upon my honor, and you both know that I mention the matter only out of regard to your own good. I will never mention it on paper again. So burn this letter, and consider me as having preached my sermon.

"The old year is dying; let its spirits be buried with its dead. Do write to me, for I'm sick and low-spirited.

"Do keep out of spirit-circles. I can't bear the idea of your sitting in the dark, squeezing other people's hands. I touch no hands but yours; press no lips but yours; think of no thoughts that I would not share with you; and do no deeds that I would conceal from you. Can you say as much? Will the spirit answer!

"Bye bye, dear Pettie! Here's a kiss for you.

"E. K. KANE."

[Dr. Kane to Miss Fox.]

"Why did you speak of 'the giraffe' to Mrs.
W——? You behaved very badly yesterday : and
I could not help feeling pained at the almost inseparable mingling of gaiety and sadness, which, poor
child, is a part of you. Maggie, be careful of 'Lish !
Sometimes I am tempted to give up friends, name,
position, honor—all for you, Maggie !

"Send word by William at what hour this evening
I may see you. But our meeting must not be misconstrued.

"Farewell.

"'Lish.

"Saturday, 3 P.M.

"Give the drawing to Dr. Bayard."

————

"The Preacher" was ever fond of moralizing;
especially on hypocrisy.

[Dr. Kane to Miss Fox.]

"Your letter was a perfect little jewel. I wil
wear it like an amulet, to guard both you and myself
from evil.

"Such letters show you in your better light, for they make me respect you. If you favored me with them oftener, you would find out by my answers how truly I watch over your happiness, and how worthy I am of the title of brother.

"Once upon a time there were certain crystal vases in Fairy Land, kept bright by the hands of 'little spirits.' When burnished they shone like the stars of heaven, and served as beacon lights to weary pilgrims afar off; but when soiled they lost their lustre and never knew brightness more.

"You would suppose that each of these fairy crystals contained some pure and beautiful object, such as young flowers kissed by dewdrops, or golden fruit just ripened on the bough. But this was not the case. In the centre of each vase, surrounded by mould and rust and mildew, was a *loathsome toad.*

"Yet in spite of this forbidding interior, so long as the 'little spirits' kept up their daily polish, so long they shone on as before; and to the weary pilgrims from afar off lost none of their brightness.

"My fairy tale—for I tell beautiful stories—would go on to say how very long, by constant labor and striving, these vases beamed; but I think you see the moral of my story, and I pause.

"Neither you nor myself give a single regretting thought to what we may carry in our own hearts. The world knows nothing of that which we all carry in our own vases; but we go on with the daily bright-

ening, and trust to the 'little spirits' that we may
always shine as beacon lights to weary pilgrims.

"There are few crystals, dear Maggie, even in fairy
land—no matter how bright or how pure they may
seem to you and me—who do not carry in their cen-
tres toads more loathsome than those of my fable."

———

The pure and constant affection of Margaret may
be seen from one of her letters, written about this
period.

[Miss Fox to Dr. Kane.]

"MY DEAR BROTHER:—I hope you were in time
for the cars yesterday morning. I have not sent
your portrait yet, but will do so during the day. It
is the most perfect likeness I ever saw of you. Mrs.
Walter, Mrs. Bayard, Dr. Bayard, Kate and I, all
go to Greenwood Tuesday, and Saturday take a short
trip with a bridal party, to be absent a few days; and
then in a short time we visit Mrs. Van Warts at
their country seat. So you see my time will be wholly
occupied for a few weeks; but I will not attempt to
tell you of any more intended pleasure-trips, as it may
be to impatient ears.

"But, my dear brother, promise me once more that

you will always love and bless me with a brotherly love; and should fate, as you say, compel us to part, will you not solemnly promise to love and think of me as your own sister!

"I am confident that our meetings are nearly at an end; but you will think of your sister often—will you not, dear Ly? and pray for her happiness?

"I have just taken my music lesson, and have more than once called my teacher 'Doctor.' I am sure, could he understand English, he would have thought I was desperately in love with some medical gentleman; but he is none the wiser, as he is an Italian, and cannot understand a word of English.

"When do you expect to be in New York again? Katie is well, and sends much love. I suppose you will be here to bid your good friend farewell before he sails for England. What a loss he will be to New York!

"From your sister
"MARGARETTA.

P. S.—I am very sorry that little Tommie bit your hand. I hope it does not give you pain. Tommie is very cross to many. You must not be superstitious, and attribute his unkindness to any fault of his mistress. Dogs are very strange things, and Tommie is very sagacious, and thinks himself *very* smart.

"MAGGIE."

Dr. Kane wrote in reply :

[Dr. Kane to Miss Fox.]

*   *   *   *   *   *   *

"Keep up your refinement by daily, patient culture. It is a quality even higher than modesty. I
know many who have the one, yet cannot attain the
other. Rub hard, 'little spirit,' at your crystal vase,
and dear Ly will help you to brighten it.

"What a dissipated lady you have become!
Greenwood with its graves on Tuesday, and wedding
parties with their brides on Saturday ! I am neither
a bride nor a corpse, so how can I catch you? On
Friday I intended to have seen you, but your list of
engagements disappointed me. When will you be
back from what you call your 'bridal party?' Perhaps that is what you mean by the 'Fates separating
us'—you are going to be a bride yourself! I can be
with you whenever you return, provided there is no
husband along with you.

"Sunday night, after ten,—or Monday morning to
breakfast—or Tuesday :—only say when : for although
I'm an obedient brother, and a faithful slave, I am
very, very busy, and cannot ride one hundred miles
to ride back again.

"With my best compliments to Tommie, believe
me, Maggie, in all confidence

"YOUR FRIEND."

"Tommie" was a favorite and ill-tempered poodle, with blue eyes; brought over from England by Miss Charlotte Cushman, the tragedienne. He had been in Miss Maggie's possession several years.

———

Mrs. Fox had several serious conversations with Dr. Kane, and strongly intimated her wish that he would abstain from visiting a young lady whom his family was not willing to receive as his wife, and who might be injured both in her feelings and her reputation by a continuance of his attentions.

Notwithstanding such rebukes, Dr. Kane continued to call—often twice and thrice a day; while in the evening he was certain to come whenever he was in New York. The matter caused much discussion among Margaret's friends, and a meeting was appointed by Mrs. Fox and Dr. Gray to consult together, as to what was best to be done.

Dr. Kane wrote as follows just before this meeting, which was to take place on the "coming Friday:"

[Dr. Kane to Miss Fox.]

"Oh, write to me, for I have no means of writing or hearing from you. I fear for the coming Friday—

fear for my friend who has no one to trust to but
me; and on Saturday I shall be in New York.
Shall I call, and if yes! at what hour! Answer by
bearer or by mail.

"Put no letters in the Post Office that are not
stamped and paid; otherwise they will not send
them."

———

The result of this consultation may be anticipated.
It was decided that no more visits should be received
from Dr. Kane under the circumstances. Margaret
was obliged to promise that she would not receive
him again, and that she would not correspond with
him. She was told that her reputation would be
injured were she to break this promise. She com-
missioned Mrs. Walter to inform Dr. Kane of her
decision, and that it was her earnest desire that they
should meet no more.

The Doctor refused to believe this. He would
never believe it, he said, unless he heard it from Margaret's own lips.

The following letter was sent to him shortly afterwards by Miss Fox.

———

"DEAR DOCTOR KANE:—I have seen you for the last time. I have been deceived. Your last interview with me has been, or will be, I know, told to Dr. G——, for Kate delights in annoying me.

"I must either give you up from this moment and for ever, or give up those who are very dear to me, and who hold my name and reputation as sacred.

"I can never see you again; but remember that you will be ever followed by my choicest love and prayers. Do not write to me, for it will only pain me. It is decided: I *cannot* see you again. You can have your letters if you wish them. No one can prevent me from returning them to you. Do as you please; if you want them, send Morton; and every letter shall be returned; but do not call on me again; for it will only give me more pain and trouble. If you have the least spark of love, or even friendship in your heart, you must not call again.

"Dr. G—— said this evening (and so did Mrs. G——) that I must refuse to see you for ever from this moment, or they would disown me. They have my promise *never to see you again*. It is a hard task for me, but I have decided. One thing do *remember*, you have my love. I believe in your honor and truth, and cannot be changed. Do not think this a mere freak of mine—mere idle words—for I am now talking to you more plainly than I have ever dared before. If, after you receive this letter, you should write to me, I would burn the letter unopened. It is now understood that you and I are never to meet again; all is over, and I have decided, I trust *wisely*.

"There is one who knows my heart; why should he think so much of this world and so little of the other? Why try to please the eyes of mortals, and overlook those eyes which are continually watching us? for the time is not distant when we will have to hear our doom; either happiness awaits us or eternal misery. And it is our privilege now to take which we please.

"I am sure we are both wise enough, and ought to spend a little while in thinking of higher things, and preparing ourselves for the change which must come sooner or later to every one on earth."

———

Part of the following was written by Dr. Kane before the receipt of the foregoing.

[Dr. Kane to Miss Fox.]

"Here I write again, dear Pet Lamb. Does not my confidence shame you? Oh, Maggie, I read you like an open book.

"Morton visits New York on Navy business; by him I send this letter. Hard work is upon me, and when I can see you who can tell? Write me often and say when.

"One of my friends sends me a bunch of winter violets. She is a pretty being, and her flowers scent my little room. By the time they reach you there will be nothing left of their fragrance. There is many a blessing which, passing from me to you, loses its soul before it reaches its heaven.

"Bye bye.

"I had written the enclosed note before I received your letter; Nevertheless I send it, Maggie, for it will show you my feelings.

"Bear up, dear little one, against your sorrows. God knows I feel more for you than for myself. Kate will not tell, and when the thing blows over we will meet again.

"You are my first care, and you do right in trusting to me. If (I cannot say it), if we really are to be rent asunder by these cursed meddlers, still, dear Maggie, we can look back upon old times and take comfort.

"I am very much distressed; very much; more than 'Little Humbug' likes to say. You say I had better not write. If this last pleasure be denied me, surely you, dear Maggie, can write to me. Oh, do this!

"As to your dear generous offer of returning my letters, I tremble—not at the letters—but at the fear

that you have not understood me. I never have distrusted you, or even asked for those notes. With
them or without them you were always the same to
me. I only felt and feared that suspicious, designing
friends or enemies might see and abuse these letters
and give me pain and trouble. I fear for them and I
fear for you. I confess that their absence makes me
unhappy; but, as I am an honorable gentleman, I
will not deprive you of them, or give you pain by
requesting them. If of your own free choice you
send them to me, I will regard it as the highest proof
of trust and love.

"But with them or without them, you shall be the
same to me. And now may God bless you, my *own
dear one!* and may you be guarded in this world to
do right! *I* will never cease to watch over you, to
love and guard you.

"E. K. KANE."

It should be noticed that Dr. Kane afterwards
refused to receive his letters, when they were offered
on several occasions. He was hurt at Margaret's wil-
lingness to part with them even to himself. Sometimes he would destroy a letter to tease her; or hide,
and afterwards return it.

XVIII.

The Doctor was in no way disposed to submit to this fiat of friends. One day calling on Mrs. W——, he insisted on her accompanying him to Tenth street, and demanded an interview with Miss Fox. Though crushed with sorrow and weeping bitterly, the poor girl was immovable in her resolution, and the Doctor acknowledged she was right. "But the world shall not say, Maggie," he cried, "that you are the discarded one! no, no—it is you who reject me! Dr. Kane is the discarded lover!" and he threw himself on his knees before the trembling and sobbing girl. "Speak, Maggie!" he continued, "my destiny is in your hands!"

Margaret replied that she would not marry him. His relations were too violently opposed to the match. It would make *him* unhappy, and she would rather part from him for ever than make him wretched in such a way!

Again and again he said to Mrs. W——, "I know her love, her goodness and purity! As far as these are concerned, I would marry her to-morrow!"

"The world's dread laugh" he might have scorned, but the distress of his family—who could not bear

the idea that his honored name should be linked with
that of one who had been, though but a few months,
associated with " spirit-rapping "—that was the obsta-
cle he dared not surmount! In the perplexity and
anguish of the hour he did not consider that the pride
which could take alarm at a silly popular prejudice
was not worth being spared. Let those who are disposed to condemn his conduct consider the circumstances in which he was placed : his present want of
pecuniary independence, his education in erroneous
ideas of social elevation, and the incessant torture
to which he was subjected from the urgent remonstrances of friends and the sneers of those indifferent
to him.

Dr. Kane continued to call frequently in Tenth
street, in spite of Margaret's refusal to see him, and
the remonstrances of her friends. They urged that
she was weak in health; the agitation she had gone
through had hurt her; and the excitement, if kept
up, would inevitably kill her. The engagement—
friendship—or whatever it was called, must be broken
off and buried for ever. Often, again and again in a
day, he went to the house and talked with Mrs. Fox,
if he could not see her daughter. He could not give
her up! he would part with life sooner! When the
mother urged that she had her child's reputation to
guard, and would rather follow her to the grave than
see her fair name tarnished, he would ask why he
could not have a brother's right to guard her fame—

to punish all who might dare assail it! He knew
her love was unchanged; his own was so; who could
watch so tenderly, so jealously over her, to banish
every thought of evil! Nothing enraged him so
much as the bare idea that unjust aspersions might
be cast upon her.

Meanwhile, reports were rife in the newspapers, as
if it were a pleasure to harpies of the press to torture
two loving hearts. The following editorial appeared
in the *New York Tribune* of November 6th, 1855 :—

"DR. KANE AND MISS FOX.

" We wish the several journals which have originated reports, *pro* and *con*, respecting the persons above
named, would consider whether they have or have
not therein perverted their columns to the gratification of an impertinent curiosity. What right has the
public to know anything about an 'engagement' or
non-engagement between these young people? If
this were a monarchy, and one or both of them were
of the blood royal, there would be an excuse for reports and speculation with regard to their relations to
each other; but in the actual state of the case, such
intimations as have appeared in the journals are not
to be justified. Whether they have been, are, may
be, are not, or will not be, 'engaged,'—can be nobody's business but their own and that of their near

relatives. Then why should the press trumpet their
names in connection with each other?" *

One evening, in a company where one of the edi-
tors of the *Daily Times* was present, the question was
brought up—as it had been in many circles—if Dr.

* The following appeared in *The Pennsylvanian* of Nov. 19th,
1855.

"DR. KANE.

"The foolish story of the engagement of Dr. Kane, the Arctic navigator, to one of the spirit-rapping Fox girls, is thus explained by a
Philadelphia correspondent of the *Boston Traveller* :—

"'Some time previous to the departure of Dr. Kane on his last
expedition, a subscription was started in New York by a number of
liberal, kind-hearted gentlemen, for the purpose of educating one of
the Fox sisters, a remarkably bright, intelligent girl, and worthy of
a better employment than 'spirit-rapping.' Dr. Kane was applied to,
and feeling somewhat interested, from pure motives of humanity
subscribed with a sailor's liberality. On his return, by invitation
of the gentleman superintending her education, he called to witness
the improvement of his protegée ; and from this simple incident has
arisen the engagement story.' "

Then followed comments upon the noble liberality of the Kane
family.

Dr. Kane cut out the above extract and read it to his Maggie with
chuckling fun, pinching her arm mischievously as "the noble liberality " of his family was mentioned.

Kane was really engaged to Miss Fox. An article
in the *Evening Post* denying that it was so "on the
best authority" was referred to. A lady present,
who was noted for her abhorrence of falsehood and
meanness, rather indignantly replied that she *knew*
there was, or had been, an engagement. The following statement appeared in the *Times* of the following
day :—

"DR. KANE'S PROSPECTS.—We are confidently assured that the Editor of *The Evening Post* has no
reason to contradict the report of the engagement of
Dr. Kane to Miss Margaret Fox."

This was followed on the succeeding day, by a
contradiction in the *Times :* "Our informant having
acknowledged that it was a mistake, &c." This contradiction had been insisted on by some party furious
in the Kane interest—who threatened vengeance
against the person who had made the assertion—could
he learn who it was; the *Times* editor having refused
to give the lady's name. On hearing this—the lady
wrote a note to Dr. Kane, acknowledging herself the
author of the statement, which she had made on
grounds amply sufficient to warrant belief. She
added, that had she heard the denial from Dr. Kane's
own lips, she would have felt bound to believe it—
as she could not conceive of a gentleman being so
cowardly or so wicked as to be influenced by fears of

the prejudices of stupid people, to repudiate an engagement to a lovely and virtuous girl. This missive, instead of irritating the Doctor by its spirited
and severe wording, elicited from him expressions of
admiration and respect. His nature was noble enough
for sympathy with generous feeling. He told the
incident to Mrs. Fox and her family, and seemed
much pleased with the sharp tone of the letter.

It was but natural that the appearance of these
cruel articles should cause indignant feeling among
the friends of Miss Fox. They blamed the Doctor
in part; for a frank avowal of the whole truth to his
friends, they thought, would have silenced the
press.

How this affected Dr. Kane may be seen from
the notes he persisted in sending.

———

[Dr. Kane to Miss Fox.]

"I have promised Mrs. W—— never to see you
again; but they tell me you have lost your confidence in me, and that, instead of leaning upon me as
a brother, you distrust me as a friend. Now I beg
you to adopt some means by which I may explain

anything which may seem to give you pain. You may command me as a brother in everything."

———

[Dr. Kane to Miss Fox.]

"Do please to see me. I have rode all night in order to comfort you, and must see you before I return."

———

[Dr. Kane to Miss Fox.]

"MY DEAR MAGGIE:—I have thought over your excellent letter, and as I seldom praise you, believe me when I say that it is with increased respect.

"I am forced to agree with you that our present meetings, I fear, must end. * *

"You always respected me; henceforward I will strive to deserve your respect.

"I accept your offered friendship, and will try and sustain you in the trial which, with true nobility of character, you have imposed upon yourself.

"On Wednesday I will see you."

———

[Dr. Kane to Miss Fox.]

" I send this note, dear Maggie, to say to you that, finding that I could not come on Wednesday, I come to-day, and leave this afternoon at four o'clock.

" Write me word at once when you can see me.

" With my regards to your mother and Katie, believe me truly,

"Your friend,

"E. K. KANE."

Thus determined was the Doctor not to be entirely deprived of the privilege of seeing or hearing from his still loved one.

Some newspaper publications drew this letter from Miss Fox, to the Doctor :

[Miss Fox to Dr. Kane.]

" I enclose two articles from the *Herald* and *Express* which have greatly distressed and worried me. Many of my friends have called (and you are aware of the position my friends hold) and requested permission to answer the articles in the newspapers. My mother has had much difficulty in preventing them from doing so. But I cannot prevent them from doing what they think just and due to me— now that they say their silence places me in a false position.

"I cannot tell you how unhappy it makes me to think of my affairs being in the mouths of so many strange persons, and the subject of newspaper comment.

"I suffer, too, on your own account; for all this talk for and against cannot fail to injure you, as well as myself. It would grieve me (you must know how much), even were we never to meet again, to hear you spoken of as a person who had no regard for his honor or his word. I am but a simple girl, and people might soon forget any idle gossip about me. But you are more widely known, and a stain on your honor would be hard to efface. I should not think of such things, believe me, but that they are forced upon my mind by what I *know* many persons say.

"I have implicit confidence in you, and trust that you will think of some right and proper means to silence all this disturbance and meddling. I believe the newspaper writers make it their business to pry into every one's business and affairs; so that we may not be able to escape their scrutiny. But neither of us should give sanction to any statement not strictly true. If we depart from the straight path, we shall be sure to suffer for it in one way or another.

"Very sincerely yours,

"MARGARET FOX.

"DR. KANE."

———

The following came with a box of bonbons from Philadelphia, at the festival season:

[Dr. Kane to Miss Fox.]

"Misses Maggie and Kate Fox, with the kind wishes of the Christmas season, from Dr. Kane.

"PHILADELPHIA, Dec. 23d, 1855.

"MISS FOX."

———

Two months later the cloud was lifted. Dr. Kane possessed the entire confidence of the family, and it was painful for them all to treat him unkindly, or to persevere in declining to receive his friendly visits. Notwithstanding the sentence of exclusion, he appears to be again on a footing of intimacy.

"FRIDAY, 1 P. M.

"MY DEAR MADAM:—I send my friend Maggie's handkerchief, which must have dropped from her muff. You see what a nice, active washerwoman I have.

"Would you do me the kindness to ask Katie at what hour precisely my sleigh shall be at your door, and to beg her and Maggie to dress warmly? I am free from engagements from four o'clock P.M.

"Very respectfully, your friend,

"E. K. KANE."

---

* * * "I think that I had better postpone seeing Mrs. W—— until my next sojourn in New York.

"I did not attend the dinner. Was Lieut. Grey there?

"E. K. KANE.

"FEBRUARY 23d, 1856."

Dr. Kane always said—and the fact cannot be doubted—that his health was seriously injured by the struggle of feeling he underwent during that winter. He would sometimes ask Margaret to put her hand upon his heart, and feel its violent and irregular beatings. But his true and constant affection was not long to be crushed under the Juggernaut wheels of unjust and absurd prejudice. It soon rose triumphant to resume its throne.

The disposition of Mrs. Fox may be seen from the subjoined letter—written apparently under the uneasiness caused by fresh gossip, or the remarks of friends on her want of firmness in still permitting interviews and letters between the partially estranged lovers.

[Mrs. Fox to Dr. Kane.]

"DR. KANE,—Dear Sir:—A letter was addressed to my daughter Margaret, which, under the circumstances, I deemed it proper to open and read. It is best for the happiness and interest of my child that you should discontinue your visits, and also leave off writing to her. My motives I hope you will understand, and respect my feelings.

"Very respectfully,
"M. FOX.

"MARCH 23d, 1856."

10*

Dr. Kane's answer was sent to Margaret:

"MY DEAR MAGGIE:—Your mother requested me not to write to you. I beg, therefore, that you will show her this letter. I have just arrived, and will see you at any hour convenient to yourself; but will not if your mother has the slightest objection. I really think, for your own sake, that I had better make this my last visit. All I think of, dear Maggie, is your reputation. As for myself, I'm only half a *gentleman ;* for they make me tell so many *stories,* that I'll be ashamed to look Mrs. E—— in the face.

"Believe me always your friend and brother,

"E. K. KANE.

"Say when by servant."

Here is an effort to return to the formal tone of a mere acquaintance·

"MY DEAR MAGGIE:—Would you do me the kindness to accept this little engraving of your Arctic friend and well-wisher? Although a mere trifle, it may serve as an evidence of my high respect for your character, and will, I hope, assure you of my continued and brotherly interest in your welfare

" With my best regards to your mother and sister, believe me your friend,

" E. K. KANE.

" FERN ROCK, April 21st, 1856.

" MISS FOX. Tenth Street.

———

Several notes of the same sort evince the writer's determination to be kept in remembrance, notwithstanding prohibitions. But it was not for long that he could enact a part foreign to his feelings.

XIX.

One day, in the latter part of April, 1856, while
Mrs. Fox was making preparations for removal to
Twenty-second street, Dr. Kane called at her house in
Tenth street, and finding Margaret was out, waited
for her return. He was sad and depressed, having
lately come from the funeral of a friend. When he
heard Margaret come in, he concealed himself behind
the parlor door, and as she entered, darted out and
clasped her in his arms. Startled at his vehemence,
the young lady strove to extricate herself; but he
only clasped her more closely, raining kisses on her
head, and crying—" My own Maggie !—you are again
mine—the betrothed wife of Dr. Kane! What more
could you ask ?"—He then took from his finger and
put on her own, a ring—memorable from having been
found in the Arctic regions—to commemorate their
renewed engagement; giving her also a locket containing the hair and initials of his deceased brother
Willie. He cared no longer—he averred—for the
world's opinion or its sneers : his beloved was all in
all to him. On this occasion he remained three or
four hours, and the joyful news was communicated to
the family, with injunctions of secrecy. When he
parted from them at the door, and went into the street,

he called out—" Now, Maggie !—Remember,"—while she held up the ring on her finger in token that she understood him.

His friend's death is referred to in a note that came soon afterwards :

———

" MY DEAR MAGGIE :—I am quite broken by my recent loss. Your letter—if you have written—has not yet been received.

"If your mother sees fit, I will call this evening. Would you oblige me by writing word if it is convenient?

"Your friend faithfully,
"E. K. KANE."

———

Miss Maggie returned the following note :

" MY DEAR DOCTOR KANE:—I should be very happy to see you this evening; but Mrs. W—— wishes me to spend the fore part of the evening with her, as she is going to have a small party. I can be home by ten, or half-past ten. If you will excuse the hour, I should be happy to see you then."

Again she wrote:

* * "I will wear your locket next my heart, and love it for ever and ever. It shall be my rosary. I'll wear it to save me from evil."

———

The young lady thus answered a letter from the Doctor sealed with green wax:

[Miss Fox to Dr. Kane.]

'Your letter, with its forsaken seal, reached me this morning. I looked for you Thursday evening, and was quite disappointed at not seeing you.

"I have received an invitation to attend a party Saturday evening; but if you will come, I will stay *at home*, as I am not very well. I have been quite ill for the last week with a severe cold on my lungs. I shall expect to see you Saturday evening, and will be disappointed if you do not come. I am also invited to attend another party Monday evening, and will go if I am well enough.

"I have more news for you: it was told me by a sincere, true friend, an editor, not a washerwoman.

"Yours sincerely,

"MARGARET FOX.

"DR. KANE."

The allusion to a "washerwoman" referred to the comments of one employed in Mrs. Fox's family, on the Doctor's lover-like behavior; with his jests thereon.

He replied to the above:

————

[Dr. Kane to Miss Fox.]

"MY DEAR MAGGIE:—I cannot meet you until Monday night, but I'm sure you do not mourn more than I do our broken tryst. No matter, my dear sister; we will think of each other until the time comes for our blessing. Watch then the lingering minutes, and await me when the shadows lengthen.

"Love to Katie and Washbosh.*

"MOSES.

"SATURDAY."

————

From this time Dr. Kane visited Maggie every day while he was in New York, and their drives and visits to places of amusement were resumed. He became playful and happy as before. One evening at the

* Col. Ashboth.

opera, where Margaret looked lovely in her blue silk and white opera cloak, he was heard to say, "As usual, I see my little Maggie has lost or forgotten her handkerchief. Here—take mine—pet lamb!" handing his to her before the company. He had rare powers of mimicry, and often convulsed his friends with laughter at his droll imitations. He would sometimes mimic the fashionable Mrs. R——, of Philadelphia. Sometimes he might be seen perched on a lofty seat, adorned with an old lady's cap and spectacles, reading a huge volume. Once, when a curious old lady was a guest of Mrs. Fox, he persuaded Margaret to tell her a great professor and lecturer was in the parlor; and forthwith commenced a discourse on abstruse scientific subjects in the most elaborate style, and in a loud tone of voice, for her edification. In such boyish pastimes he delighted, and his return to them showed a heart once more at ease.

Some little time before, when Miss Kate was holding a private circle, of which one was a homœopathic physician, the Doctor proposed a practical joke, and wrote out the following spirit oracles :—

"Let not the doctrine which was conceived in toil, rear a giant growth of ignorance and miscomprehension."

"*Similia* refer not to things which are in themselves the same, but to those alike by sympathies."

"Study remedies *ab initio;* for it matters not to

augment a force where we know not the agent of pro-
pulsion."

Miss Maggie, however, protested against the joke
being played out.

The wonted shower of notes and letters recom-
menced; most of them written in haste, amid pressing labors, and hardly illustrative enough for publication in this memoir.   One or two will suffice.

————

[Dr. Kane to Miss Fox.]

"DEAR MAGGIE:—I know I ought to be in Philadelphia, but I really cannot bear to leave.

"Yet I fear you have some engagement to-night,
which you cannot postpone.

"Send word if you wish me to stay, and at what
hour I must be with you.   Tell Mrs. F—— that my
one good answer last night makes me anxious to try
again.

"If you are engaged, do say so.   Always be at
home with Elish'.   Do whatever pleases you best."

————

It is probable the following refers to some idle gossip, or fears concerning it:—

" MY DEAR MAGGIE :— * * * I am not nervous, but you *must* write to me. Write, I say ; write at once. I cannot come on to see you. I will not come until you distinctly tell me in your letter that you wish me to come—and say when you will be disengaged. Excuse me, my little Maggie, if I am abrupt ; but I never loved you better than at this moment ; and, if you are what I hope you are, you will like me the better for this hurried, truthful letter. Read every word of it to Katie ; take her advice, and write at once to me.

"E. K. KANE."

" I will call at seven, and if Mrs. Fox has no objection, take you and Kate to the Lecture. I suppose, as Electricity is the subject, he will say nothing about spirits.

" Write word by bearer if seven o'clock suits."

In several notes like the following he joked with Miss Kate :—

[Dr. Kane to Miss Kate Fox.]

" DEAR KATE :—Tell your mother that I think that I had better not go to the theatre with you, but I will call up with my questions this evening at six o'clock. Tell Maggie not to laugh, but to treat the matter gravely, and apologize to your mother for the trouble which I gave her last evening.

" I was just about to leave town.

" Very faithfully, your friend,

" E. K. KANE.

" MISS FOX.   " Tuesday."

———

In the house occupied by Mrs. Fox in Twenty-second street, Maggie had a prettily furnished parlor on the third floor, where Dr. Kane and she sometimes sat, when strangers were expected in the family parlor, or when Miss Kate had a " circle." Mrs. Fox on one occasion objected to the Doctor's entering this room, on account of its being out of order. He wrote the next day :—

[Dr. Kane to Miss Fox.]

" I start in a few minutes, but cannot leave without sending you a drop of comfort, and thanking you for a most delightful evening.

"Tell your mother not to distress herself about the third story room. I regard it as a sort of sanctuary: a retreat to which we are driven by mischief-making eyes and tongues. There, like wounded deer, we escape from the hunters; and if we, both of us, are conscious of doing no wrong, whose business is it if we seek a shelter? Nevertheless, dear Maggie, I want to be very careful, and cannot bear to give you a moment's pain or care. When we see each other again I will be very good, and you will remember me with the respect of a brother.

"We are friends now.

"Bye bye.

"Write me an answer if this comes safely to you."

———

This was left on the table one day:

[Dr. Kane to Miss Fox.]

"Eleven o'clock.

"DEAR MAGGIE:—I have waited long and wearily in the little third story room, and now I hie me back to my solitary home.

"Where there is no confidence there can be no warmer feeling. I do not know where you spend

the evening, but I know that you will sleep none the
sounder for having given pain to your friend and
brother."

———

The following seems to be in reply to some letter of
Margaret's that gave pain or displeasure, and shows
the kind of logic by which the Doctor must have
quieted his conscience when it charged him with tri-
fling or inconsistency.

[Dr. Kane to Miss Fox.]

"DEAR MAGGIE :—You see that, as in old times, I
confide in you and write. So much for my inability
to say ' no ' to you. You asked for a letter—be-
hold it !

"Where shall I begin? Will you have a long
story? 'The History of the Spirit Rappers '—or one
of my queer wild tales of Norman Knights and
Weeping Vestals? Suppose I begin thus :—

"Once in the mornings of old, I read in a penny
newspaper that for one dollar the inmates of another
world would rap to me the secrets of this one; the
deaths of my friends, the secret thoughts of my sweet-
hearts; all things spirit-like and incomprehensible

would be resolved into hard knocks, and all for
one dollar! 'Strange!' thought I; 'so much for
so little! all this for one dollar! I'll go and see
them!'

" With that, all alone I wended my way to a hotel,
and after the necessary forms of doorkeepers and
tickets—by Jove, I saw the 'spirit.'

" Here let me stop, dear Maggie, for I write to
please and not to pain you. Will you, dear darling,
in whom I so truly trust that my very honor is in
your keeping—will you look back upon those old
days (when you paraded yourself on glass tumblers
at a dollar a head*) and upon these; upon yourself,
dear Maggie, as you are now? Can you help feeling
that you are in every respect better than you were
then; more truthful, more innocent, more pure;
better friends around you, and a wiser and purer path
ahead?

" When people speak badly of me and I for your
sake bear it, ask yourself the question: 'Has not
Elisha done his best to make me a happier and a
better girl? Has he ever deceived me? Has he not
always said to me openly, and as a gentleman, that
some day I should be his wife; that in *all, all* he is
mine?'

" Maggie, I have had but one thought, how to

---

* The medium was thus insulated, to see if electricity had aught
to do with the phenomena.

make you happier. How to withdraw you from *a deception;* from a course of sin and future punishment, the dark shadow of which hung over you like the wing of a vampire. Have I not, dear darling, striven to elevate and raise you to my own standing? Maggie, Maggie, when you are tempted to forget old times, and false friends misrepresent me, go and read this letter, and see if for many years I have not proved myself a true, self-sacrificing friend and lover.

"I am working hard here, but the three weeks will soon pass. Even while at my student's desk, pondering over matters too dull for your bright brain, thoughts, sweet thoughts, distress me.

"Write soon. Bye bye.

"Here goes my name,

"E. K. KANE.

"P. S.—Write at once, and do explain your strange letter. It looks as if you distrusted me—or else as if I ought to distrust you."

XX.

-"The course of true love" still ran over occasional roughnesses that caused now and then flashes of foam. Some bit of gossip repeated to Mrs. Fox draws from her a severe letter to the Doctor, which he thus acknowledged:

[Dr. Kane to Mrs. Fox.]

"MY DEAR MRS. FOX:—I received, with deep mortification and surprise, your recent letter. I do not know what has occurred since we all met so happily around your little table; but I have too much respect for your wishes not to follow your request.

"As to dear Maggie, I cannot bear the thought of having unintentionally injured one for whom I have so high a regard. She will always be in my eyes entitled to that respect which her character deserves; and it will be my privilege, as well as duty, to defend her from any aspersion which may be cast upon her.

"May I beg you, as an act of justice to myself, to show this letter to your daughters, that they may learn how I have acceded to your wishes? Tell them, but especially tell Maggie, that this matter has caused me much pain; but that they may still regard me as a friend, taking a warm and brotherly interest in their welfare.

" With much respect, I am, Madam,
    " Very faithfully
        " Your friend and ob't servant,
                        " E. K. KANE.

"PHILADELPHIA, June 24th, 1856.

" MRS. MARGARET FOX,
    "22d Street,
        "New York."

If the phrase " brotherly interest " provoke a smile from the reader, it often did not less from the Doctor himself, when he glanced over his missives, or was reminded of the terms he had used. But it was hardly misapplied, for, as three years before, much of paternal tenderness had been blended with his love for the young girl he wished to educate, there was now much of the brotherly feeling in the attachment that governed his actions. The young lady seems to have had a partiality for this fraternal bond; for her letters have more or less the tone of a loving sister, while the Doctor occasionally evinces a preference for that mode of address,—as follows:

"DEAR SISTER MAGGIE:—Pity me! I'm truly worn out with hard work, and have lost quite a large sum of money. I long for a holiday where I can cease to play great man, and play the fool instead.

"Keep my money loss a secret except to your mother. These are things better never spoken of; but I wish I had the *filthy lucre* cut up into silk dresses, or even swallowed in sugar-plums; anything better than being cheated. Tell your mother that it is worse than gaslights and *washbosh*.

"Nearly all my private affairs, somehow or other, find their way to your ears. I trust you a great deal more than I ought to; but I never speak of the affairs of others, for those do not belong to me.

"I cannot come until Tuesday, and then not until ten o'clock. I start again at six in the morning; so that our happy moments will be few, and purchased on my part by a ride of two hundred miles. Do keep yourself disengaged; for no spirits, terrestrial, heavenly, or infernal, must come between you and your friend.

"By this time I had expected to have turned your little bedchamber into a flower-garden; but I am so very, very busy—no matter; there's an end to all labor, and we will both enjoy more the rest when it comes.

"Good-bye, dear Maggie; there is not a single

naughty word, and what is better, not a single naughty thought in all this letter. Think often of me, and expect me on Tuesday night.

"Bye bye.

"LY."

The "rest" spoken of, must have been the completion of the Doctor's book, which he was working hard to finish and get through the press. Its success would give him the independence he craved.

Miss Maggie was in the habit of stigmatizing as ' naughty " every species of teazing reproof or vexing complaint from her friend ; and he often playfully used the word as she meant it.

Here is her reply. The flowers came later.

[Miss Fox to Dr. Kane.]

" MY .DEAREST :—Your letter reached me this morning. Then you are doomed to pass another day in Philadelphia. It is now five days since you left, and it seems a whole year to me. Oh, my lover and friend, hasten ! My hours grow irksome when you stay so long !

"The roses have not yet arrived. I shall look for them to-morrow.

" The cover is beautiful, and the things are as you left them, save your portrait. I have placed it over my bed, that I might look upon it until I fall asleep.

My parlor is pleasant; still, the lamps burn dimly when you are not here.

"The evenings are growing cold, and I have written this letter in my thin wrapper; but I can never take cold in doing anything for you—my dearest friend.

"To-morrow you will be here! How happy the thought of seeing you makes me! Oh, my star! I live but to love you!

"You frightened me, my love. I hope you are better. If not, send for me, and I will come to you!

"And now, my star! my saint! my only soul!

"Farewell.

"MAGGIE.

"Midnight.
     E. 22d St."

———

Miss Margaret sent to her lover-friend a work of Sir Robert Owen, sent to her by a friend from England, and never republished in this country. The book had reached Crookville while Margaret was at school, and she was permitted to read it; a permission not granted in the case of the *Tribune*, or any spiritualist publication.

Maggie was in the habit of playfully calling Dr. Kane's family "the royal family;" hence his allusion.

" *Ante-script.*

" P.S.—*En Avance.*

" Here is an old times letter. I'm sure you hardly deserve one. Do write at once.

"DEAR MAGGIE:—The Royal Family keep me in our quiet city to attend a ball; and on Friday I have to talk science and stupidity to a society of learned philosophers. Pity me, for truly I had rather be with you, resting after my hard work like a boy in his holiday time. Even if you were as cross as you are kind, it would be a pleasure to be shut out from the big world, gazing at your dark eyes and pouting lips. How much more a pleasure is it to do more than gaze !

" On Saturday I shall be in New York; or if not Saturday—Monday. I shall bring with me the picture [the portrait of Judge Kane] which you desire; but do, dear Maggie, be careful of it. I have every confidence in you, but *none* in your discretion. I know that you respect me none the less because I guard my truthfulness. I am not as good as I ought to be; but next to guarding and loving you, I most regard my own word. Don't be angry with dear Elish' for telling you this. I respect your *pride*, and want this uncharitable world to respect both it and you.

" Bye bye."

It will be seen that he was hardly yet prepared to meet the censure of his friends for having again plighted his faith to one to whom the odium of "the spirit-rappings" still clung, notwithstanding that her abhorrence of the association was now as deep as his own. He once observed to a friend, that no poverty or obscurity could have stood for a moment in the way of his marriage with Miss Fox. But the abominable rappings! how could he link his name with them!

The subjoined letter, like many others, has no date.

"My Own Dear Pet Lamb—When I think over our last happy evening, I fear that it may lessen me in your respect. I hasten, therefore, of my own accord, to ask you to forgive me. Indeed, dear Maggie, I was carried away by my own tempei, and you must not let its force make you think that I undervalue your own delicacy and ladylike refinement. Now, that I am away from you, I would give worlds for the simple pleasure of sitting by your side, listening to riddles, and telling stories of ancient days.

*   *   *   *   *   *   *   *

*   *   You were, and always shall be, *my own dear little Maggie.*   There now !

"Write to me if I shall come on Thursday, at five o'clock. I will do exactly as you desire, and would not for the world, in order to please myself by seeing you, run a risk of making trouble or regret. The locket I will bring with me.

"I've something very curious to tell you   *   *   *

*   *   *   *   *   *   *   *

"And now, dear Maggie, good-night. Read this letter over as you go to bed, and imagine dear Elish' patting your hands, or pressing his rough beard against your glowing cheeks. Don't think of me as the wicked person that I have learned to be since I came to this uncharitable land of Mrs. E——s and Doctor G——s ; but as dear Lye, the friend of old times, who never advised you in all his life to do wrong, or did wrong himself, if he could help it."

*   *   *   *   *   *   *   *

———

Dr. Kane was always anxious to impress on his lady-love the importance of punctuality and careful exactness in the smallest matter. One day when he called and found her absent, Miss Kate informed him she had promised to return "in three minutes." The Doctor took out his watch, and finding the three minutes extended to ten, he read the young lady a lecture. He would sometimes ask her if such or such an article of furniture was in such a place in another room; and when a random answer was given, would ascertain if it were so, and read a severe homily if it were not, on the culpability involved in that kind of carelessness.

He would not permit her even to witness any spiritual manifestation, nor to remain in the room when the subject was discussed. One evening, when Miss Kate had a circle sitting in the parlor, the Doctor walked with Margaret through the hall; and as they passed the open door, he drew her head aside, and held up his arm as if to shield her from the sight. "You shall never be brought into contact with such things again—my child"—he would say.

His jealous care to guard her from the knowledge of all that could contaminate, was at all times remarkable. Once in a sleigh-ride on the Bloomingdale road, rather late in the afternoon, they drove near a hotel resorted to by pleasure-parties. There was a riotous crowd of men and women singing a drinking song at the door and on the long piazza. Without saying a word, Dr. Kane rose in the sleigh, and

threw the buffalo skin over Margaret's head, keeping
it there till they had passed the place.   He could not
bear that she should look upon such a scene.

11*

XXI.

The following missive from Miss Maggie was sent shortly before her summer trip to Canada:

[Miss Fox to Dr. Kane.]

"I have just received an invitation to dine Thursday evening with some eighteen or twenty ladies and gentlemen at one of those Fifth Avenue mansions that we were so much enamored with during our yesterday's drive. I shall dress in the pale blue silk; the very color of your friend Mrs. G——'s cap-strings; I mean ribbons—excuse me! I shall wear blue silk to please my Elish', for I know he has a passion for that sweet color. You see that 'poor 'Lish' is not the only one who honors 'Miss Margaret Fox.'

"When shall we have the pleasure of seeing you and your handsome brother? Please write to me by return of mail, and let me know that you are well and happy.

"Yours in the sincerity of love,

"MARGARET FOX."

One evening, when Miss Margaret was at a party
at the Hon. John Cochrane's, Dr. Kane called to say
good-bye, and left the following:

[Dr. Kane to Miss Fox.]

"Oh, Maggie, why were you not here? I have
waited two weary hours. You do not trust me.

"I have telegraphed—so that I must leave; but if
you love me, write and comfort your attached friend,
brother, everything!

"God bless you!"

———

Perhaps as much of individual character may be
read in such brief missives as in longer epistles. Dr.
Kane had no time for letter-writing. His biographer
says, "The unanswered letters which crowded around
him might well appal an abler man."

[Dr. Kane to Miss Fox.]

"Maggie, I am in town, but leave to-morrow.
Are you well and happy? You have not written to
me."

On another occasion a similar complaint was made. The young lady had gone to call on a friend, and had neglected her engagement:

[Dr. Kāne to Miss Fox.]

"DEAR MAGGIE:—I have waited my two long hours, and I leave you sorry and grieved at your distrust. Where there is no confidence there can be no friendship.

"Bye bye."

"I'm tired of waiting.

"Good-bye. Will you ride? I will bring carriage in half an hour."

"Send a note by the bearer.

"Will you be in and disengaged this afternoon? If so, at what hour?"

[Dr. Kane to Mrs. Fox.]

"MY DEAR MAGGIE:—The gentleman who owns the wonderful stove—is no gentleman at all. He is an old maid. He did me the honor to say that his stove was the only one in the country, and that he would part with it neither for love nor money. In vain I urged all my eloquence; in vain said that bright eyes would glow over its mysterious flames, and sweet lips close like kisses over its delectable dishes. The wretch was inexorable. Finally I told him that I wanted it for my sister; whereupon, to the credit of human nature, he relented, and gave me the whole curiosity shop at cost. So you see that if I did not consider you as my sister, we would have had no stove. May we have many merry suppers over it, and many laughs at its history !

"By the blessing of railroad cars, I will return from Virginia on Saturday, and if things suit in Twenty-second street, take supper with you on Monday. Could I come round in the afternoon? Do write me a letter saying if convenient. Of course I expect to cook my own supper and yours.

"Many kind wishes to you, dear Maggie, and to your family. Tell Katie to drink no champagne, and do you follow the same advice. It makes your nose red, and is a bad custom for young ladies, unless in the company of medical men or grave preachers. With my respects to Mrs. Fox, believe me

"YOUR FRIEND."

The stove described was to be used with an alcohol lamp, for cooking purposes.

Mrs. Fox and Margaret fixed a day in August for their departure for Canada, on a visit to relatives. Dr. Kane gave the young lady many cautions. " You must remember," he said, " that you are mine ; you must hold yourself sacred, as my wife should be ; there must be no flirting ; you must receive no attentions from gentlemen."

" Shall'I then disclose our engagement ? " was her laughing question. " Yes—if brought to it," was his reply.

Margaret wrote from Rochester :

[Miss Fox to Dr. Kane.]

" MY DEAREST LY :—We left New York Thursday morning at half-past five, and went as far as Syracuse, where the cars halted for a few minutes. Mother got out in the mean time to attend to her baggage, and before she could possibly get back, the cars were off, and our dear mother was left behind. Three more distracted girls than Katie, Emma, and I, were never known ; perfectly unacquainted with travel-

ling, and then we were destitute of one penny to pay
our passage. What to do, we did not know. The
conductor and passengers were very kind, and did all
in their power to comfort us.

"As soon as we arrived at Rochester, we went to
a very fine hotel near the depôt. They told us that
there was another train at half-past seven. We com-
posed ourselves as much as possible, and were all at
the depôt at seven precisely. The cars arrived punctually at the hour mentioned; but our mother was
not there. We went back perfectly crazy. We
waited anxiously for the next train, which was
expected at half-past nine; but mother did not come
until the next day. You can imagine how perfectly
happy we were when she came, and how careful we
were not to let her get off the cars again without us.
We will go from here to * * *"

––––––

The next letter of Dr. Kane speaks for itself. It
may have been written before the receipt of the
above.

[Dr. Kane to Miss Fox.]

"Written Monday, Aug. 24th, in third story front
room, 22d street. The house dark and solitary.

"I do not know whether you will ever receive this letter; for Mary* has to get the address from ——, and I trust to her to direct it for me.

"Why, you funny little Tutie, did you not send me word where you were about to rest your wandering footsteps? Your letter was a charming one, but that it came too late for a Newark answer, and you gave me no means of replying anywhere else.

"Give my best regards to your mother and Kate. Say that I miss them very much, and that during my New York visits, the wretched hotels, with their crowds of company, form a poor substitute for the quiet rest of their hospitable homestead. Most of all do I miss you; the third story room seems desolate without you. Always I think of you with brotherly affection—always with respect.

"Tommy is a spoiled child; if he is killed, it will be with kindness. Mary has *carte blanche* at the butcher's, and he eats of the fat of the land. Even now I hear him barking—I suppose at my picture; and although he is as fat and as amiable as ever, I think that he misses you. Strange to say, he takes quite kindly to me, and licks my hand as if we ought to be good friends, because we had the same mistress. If he could speak, he would say,—'You think yourself a great man, but she loves me more than she loves you, and she never beats mè or pulls my nose.'

* The servant.

"Mary is well. She tells me that Mrs. —— was here yesterday and to-day, with her assiduous and venerable friend from Chicago. ——, too, is well. Mrs. W—— I have not seen, but will call upon soon.

"Much as I miss you, I would not advise your return before you can possibly help it. Certainly, not before the third or fourth of September. Your health, and your mother's and sister's, is of more importance than Kate's spiritual *pow-wow* in this hot city. I myself am very sick, and go this afternoon to *Brattleboro'*, *Vermont*, to which address send me a letter at once, saying when you will be back; what is your mother's health, and above all, dear Maggie, whether I can be of any use to you. Say this to your mother; she will understand me; and be assured that I make the offer in the sincerity of a long-tried friendship.

"This may seem to you a cold letter; but remember that strange eyes may see it, for it may never reach you. The best answer to all your fears is to show you the caution with which I guard you and your name. Should a passing thought of sorrow come to you on my account, I would never forgive myself. Except for words of praise, my tongue shall be as a sealed book.

"But just to think of it! You will see me again before I cross the water, for I cannot leave until the tenth; and as soon as your letter reaches me, will hasten to New York. There I will meet you as a sister, and part from you as from one who has the highest possible claim to my brotherly affection and honorable regard.

" There, ' Toots.' "

————

The following, written by moonlight in Canada, must have been received with transport by the absent lover.

[Miss Fox to Dr. Kane.]

" It is late, my beloved, and I have carefully stolen from my bed, that I might write to you undisturbed even by the breathings of others. It is after midnight, and the sweet moon is the only witness to my devotion.

" For four days I have done nought but weep. How has our separation affected you? I am very gloomy. Without you all is darkness, and every place seems a grave. You ask if I mix in company? No, no! I join no merry scenes. *Lish'*, I have not laughed since we parted. By the time we meet again I fear I shall quite have forgotten to laugh; and then you will clothe me in the habiliments of a nun, and send me to a convent to count my rosary.

" On the wings of angels I send you ten thousand
kisses.

" Bye bye.

" MAGGIE.

" Morning is nearly upon me."

———

[Miss Fox to Dr. Kane.]

"MELVILLE, CANADA WEST, Sept. 1st, 1856.

" I have purposely delayed writing to you, my
dearest, in the hope that I should have the pleasure
of seeing you once more before your departure for
England.   But I fear it will be impossible, as we shall
not be able to reach New York before the middle or
last of next month.   It is only three weeks since we
left New York, yet it seems much longer.

" Have you visited our home in Twenty-second
street?   I suppose if you have you found it solitary
enough.

" We think of leaving the Canadian shores about
the 17th of September.

" It is growing late, and I have just time to return
my grateful thanks for the kind and brotherly interest
that you have always manifested for me.   Wishing
you a happy journey and a safe return,

" Believe me, with much love,

" Yours devotedly,

"MARGARET FOX.

"P. S.—I have often dreamt of you since I left, and have twice dreamt that you were very, *very* ill; and I waked each time weeping bitterly. But fortunately my dreams always prove false, unless they are of an agreeable character.

"I am no great believer in dreams, whether pleasant or unpleasant.

"MAGGIE."

[Miss Fox to Dr. Kane.]

"I hope, my dearest Ly, that you are much better than when I left you. I suppose in a few days you will be on your way to England. How long will you remain in England? We would have visited my brother before going to Canada, had it not been for mother's being left.

"I should love much, my dear brother, to have you write to me, but fear that your letters may not reach us, as we will be travelling nearly all the time. I wrote from Rochester, and requested Mr. Smith to keep all letters safely that came directed either for my mother, Kate, or myself, until we visited Arcadia, which would be within one month. Therefore, if you have written to me, the letter will be kept perfectly safe until I receive it.

" The weather is very cool and pleasant ; rather too cool. I will direct this letter to your handsome brother Patterson. 'It's very artistic, Mrs. Fox.' He must have thought me exceedingly rude ; but it was perfectly impossible for me to suppress my laughter.

"I remember your promise while with Mr. ——. You know that my opinion of that gentleman is rather poor. Perhaps if I knew more of his good qualities I should respect him more.

" Mother and Kate send their love to you. Think of me, and believe me ever

" Devotedly yours,
"MARGARET FOX.

" P. S.—I wish that you would please go to our house, and request Mary (the servant girl) to put little Tommie in a room above, and keep my door locked all the time, so that —— cannot read my letters. I wish that you would take my key and keep it until you go to England. Please do this ; for there are many letters that I would not for worlds —— should read."

————

The key was that of the room containing the box which held all the letters of Dr. Kane to Miss Fox. The key of the box itself had been consigned to the

Doctor's charge when Margaret went to Canada. He could have taken away all his letters had he chosen to do so. This fact may serve to show the perfect confidence subsisting between the lovers. Dr. Kane often seemed to think of the possibility of his love-letters being published. He would say—intimating that something might happen at a future time to render a publication necessary—" Maggie, never fear, you hold a fortune in my letters." He at all times expressed a wish that they should be ever in her keeping; and sometimes reproved her for not being careful enough of them.

XXII.

A letter of Dr. Kane's bids his friend direct to Stockbridge, Massachusetts. As the time drew near when he expected her, he requested that a note might be sent to him at the Brevoort House, New York, where he was ill, as soon as the party arrived from Canada. Almost every hour of the day preceding their return, he rang the bell of the house in Twenty-second street, and he was with them five minutes after they came, with a delighted welcome. He breakfasted with them the next morning, and had a long conversation upon the future. This was some two weeks before the time fixed for the Doctor's departure for England, whence he expected to be back in the spring. At this time Dr. Kane appeared willing to defy the severest censures of the class of persons aptly designated as "snobs." He seemed to glory in his devotion to the object of his love. He had the volumes of his work bound to order for her, and almost every day brought her some token of regard. He told her of a diamond bracelet he had ordered at Tiffany's, and added, smiling, as they drove there for it—" They will all know now, Maggie, that I want it for my betrothed."

On first entering her own little parlor in the house, Margaret saw the following billet, in the Doctor's hand-writing, pinned up so as to meet her eye:

"God bless you, dear Maggie! I have tried to do all that I could during your absence, to show my brotherly regard. Have trust in me always. Write under cover to my brother as soon as you arrive. Remember me to your mother and Kate."

Dr. Kane was always exceedingly particular in keeping appointments, and in apologies whenever prevented from doing so; also in consulting the convenience of others in making them. These little notes illustrate this trait.

[Dr. Kane to Mrs. Fox.]

"MY DEAR MADAM:—I am suffering so much that I cannot leave my bed; if, therefore, I should be unable to pay my respects to-day, I pray you to accept my apologies.

"Your obedient servant,
"E. K. KANE."

[Dr. Kane to Mrs. Fox.]

"MY DEAR MADAM:—The train does not leave
as I expected. Ask Maggie if she can see me
before I leave town, and send me word when, by the
bearer.

"Truly your friend,
"E. K. KANE.

"I must leave to-morrow morning early."

———

[Dr. Kane to Miss Fox.]

"DEAR MAGGIE:—I have but a minute to show,
by an accidental chance, that I still remember you.
Be all that I would wish you. Remember my advice,
and you will be always with me that which you have
been and are.

" God bless you, my dear, darling little ' spirit! '
" Good-bye.

"E. K. KANE."

———

At one of their partings about this time, Maggie
took her locket, containing Willie's hair, and attached
it to the Doctor's guard-chain, to be worn during his
absence abroad. She little thought that, like the ring
noticed, it would be kept from her after his death.

12

Many verses were addressed by Doctor Kane to his betrothed, which prove him a far better navigator than poet.

> "Purely though I love her, and worship none above her,
> Madly as I adore her, and sadly as I bore her,"

(to use his own words) the reader would scarcely pardon the lack of poetic merit for the ardent expression of his unbounded love. One of his metrical effusions was a prayer which he directed Maggie to "learn by heart, and say it when you go to bed at night." In this curious production devotional aspiration has hardly the preëminence over the worship he craved for himself from the chosen of his heart. He wished to have all her thoughts at all times. The "prayer," like numerous poems indited by the lover, must be consigned to oblivion.

A very short time before Dr. Kane sailed, he took Margaret to the opera at Niblo's. Several ladies and gentlemen were in the private box opposite. The Doctor asked Maggie to look and tell him what she thought of them—if they were really well-bred persons. When she answered in the negative he laughed heartily, and said he thought her opinion correct.

One day he took from a basket of fruit on Mrs. Fox's table some bunches of grapes, wove them into a garland, and placed it on Margaret's head, bidding her remember that she was his wife—solemnly pledged in the sight of Heaven—and ere long to be such in the face of the world. This acknowledgment had been once before made, when the parties were alone.

One evening the Doctor came to Twenty-second street, weary and low-spirited, and was told that Margaret was not at home "Is it possible!" he cried—"when she knew I was coming—and only a day or two before I must leave her, too!" He took a seat with a look of deep disappointment, when a closet door flew open, and out sprang the young lady, blooming and laughing, very coquettishly dressed, and more beautiful than he had ever seen her. Matters were then arranged for a drive next morning to have her ambrotype taken.

He wrote out the description as follows :

"Ambrotype—Large plate—Figure erect — complete Profile—Eyelids drooping—Countenance pensive and looking down."

In the morning came this note, sent either by Morton or Mr. Grinnell, who had been the bearer of many missives :

[Dr. Kane to Miss Fox.]

"DEAR TUTIE:—I fear that the weather is too cloudy. I will be at No. 50 at half-past eleven o'clock, when, if it clears up, you can drive down and meet your mother at 'the rooms.' Mention this to her, with my best respects, and send me word if the plan suits you."

———

Immediately afterwards the following :

[Dr. Kane to Miss Fox.]

"DEAREST PET:—Do dress at once, and have the ambrotype taken. I will come up in less than an hour and see to your costume. Don't be afraid of your neck and shoulders. I want you to look like a Circe, for you have already changed me into a wild Boar.

"VALE."

———

Shortly before his departure, Dr. Kane came to tea, and spent the evening, as usual, with his beloved.

Reclining on the sofa, he talked despondingly of what might happen in his absence. His health was precarious; he might be ill; he might die. "If I send for you, my own Maggie, will you come to me?" he asked. "Certainly I will," she answered. "I fear you would hesitate," he murmured; "and yet you know you are my own—my wife! You remember what I have told you!" A moment afterwards he added—"Would you like me to repeat what I have said, formally, in the presence of your mother? Such a declaration, in the presence of witnesses, is sufficient to constitute a legal and binding marriage; a marriage as firm as if the ceremony took place before a magistrate.* Attend to me, Maggie; listen; would you be willing *now* to enter into such a bond?"

---

* "No peculiar ceremonies are requisite by the common law to the valid celebration of the marriage. The consent of the parties is all that is required; and as marriage is said to be a contract *jure gentium*, that consent is all that is required by natural or public law."

KENT'S COMMENTARIES, *Vol.* II., *page* 53.

"It is very clear that the marriage contract is valid and binding if made by words *de præsenti*, though it be not followed by cohabitation."

M'Adam v. *Walker*, 1 *Dow's Rep.* 148.

Jackson v. *Winne*, 7 *Wendell*, 47 *and* 50. Note (a) and cases there cited.

"The consent of the parties may be declared before a magistrate,

At this moment Miss Katharine Fox came into the room.   Dr. Kane desired her to call her mother, who came up stairs to the parlor; the servant, and a young

or simply before witnesses, or subsequently confessed or acknowledged."

KENT'S COM., *Vol.* II., *p.* 55.

" If the contract be made *per verba de presenti,* and remains without cohabitation (or if made *per verba de futuro,* and be followed by consummation), it amounts to a valid marriage in the absence of all civil regulations to the contrary, and to which the parties (being competent as to age and consent) *cannot dissolve,* and is equally binding as if made *in facie ecclesiæ.*"

II. KENT'S COM., *5th Ed., pp.* 53 *and* 54.

"Marriage is a civil contract, and all that is essential to its validity is a *present agreement* between competent parties, to take each other for husband and wife; and this agreement may, like any other fact, be proved either by direct or circumstantial evidence."

Clayton and Wife v. *Wardell et al., Executors, &c.; 4 Comst. R.* 230.

NEW YORK COURT OF APPEALS.

"Nothing more is necessary than a full, free, and mutual consent between the parties, though there be no consummation."

Jackson v. *Winne,* 7 *Wend.* 47.

THE REVISED STATUTES OF NEW YORK, 5th Edition, Vol. III., page 229, after an article relating to the solemnization and proof of marriages, says .

" Nor shall the provisions of this article be construed to require the parties to any marriage, or any minister or magistrate, to solemnize the same in the manner herein prescribed; but all lawful marriages contracted in the manner heretofore in use in this State shall be as valid as if this article had not been passed."

In the case of the People v. Hayes, tried in the Court of General Sessions, and the judgment affirmed in the Supreme Court, in 1863, lady who was spending the evening there, being also present. Dr. Kane informed them he had sent for them to witness the solemn declaration that would follow. Then, standing up, and holding Margaret's hand, while his left arm encircled her form, he said: " Maggie is my wife, and I am her husband. Wherever we are, she is mine, and I am hers. Do you understand and consent to this, Maggie? " Margaret answered that she did.

Dr. Kane then explained that he had wished to say this before witnesses, to provide against anything that might happen before they could meet again. A very near relative of his own, he said, had been privately married a long time before it was in any manner made public. Again he assured his beloved that the ceremony which had just passed, made them as

the Recorder charged the jury that in this State there may be a valid marriage, though not formally solemnized before a clergyman, or consent declared before a magistrate. If parties, competent to contract, in the presence of witnesses, agree together to be husband and wife, it is a legal marriage.

The Court of Appeals held that the essence of the contract, as of all contracts, is the consent of the parties; and its validity does not depend upon any form of celebration, nor the fact of cohabitation. The consent of parties, without any peculiar forms or ceremonies, is all that is required to its valid celebration.

This case was reported in 25th New York Reports, page 390.

(Reeve's Domestic Relations, 3d Edition, p. 196 and note. Starr *v.* Peck, 1 Hill, 270; Fenton *v.* Read, 4 Johns. 52; Clayton *v.* Wardwell, 4 Comst. 230; Bishop on Mar. and Div. Chap. V.)

indissolubly one as if performed in a church. "It shall be made public in May," he added.

The day previous Dr. Kane had taken Margaret with him to make farewell calls. They called at General Scott's, Judge Blunt's, Mrs. Wood's, and other places, leaving cards of adieu.

The brief note below was to prepare Mrs. Fox for an evening visit:

[Dr. Kane to Mrs. Kane.]

"I take a farewell dinner with the officers; after which, if acceptable to you, I will pay my respects to your mother and yourself. Will seven o'clock find you at home?"

———

[Dr. Kane to Mrs. Kane.]

"DEAR WIFE:—May I meet you at half-past ten to-night? I have a capital excuse for your mother. Do not say *no*, but send word the earliest hour, and I'll be with you."

XXIII.

During the last evening, Dr. Kane seemed oppressed by gloomy forebodings. "Maggie, what if I should die away from you !"—he exclaimed, in anguish. "Oh, my own Maggie, could I but die in your arms, I would ask no more !" Again: "I can part from all the rest,—even from my mother—with calmness:—it is parting with you, Maggie, that kills me !" He stayed late. Morton came for him just after he had gone, and received Maggie's injunctions.

"Remember, Morton—take good care of the Doctor"—were her parting words to him. "That I will, Miss Maggie"—was his reply.

On one occasion, months before, Dr. Kane had said to Mrs. W——: "I fear Maggie does not love me; poor child, it is not in her nature !"—He did not now doubt her love. He clasped the diamond bracelet on her arm, and bade her wear it for his sake who loved her with his whole soul. He gave her several envelopes lined with muslin, which he had directed to himself, that her letters enclosed therein might go with safety. One of these, addressed to the care of Bowman, Grinnell & Co., Liverpool, he marked curiously with stars on the inside corners. This private mark, not understood by any of his family, was to signify Maggie's wish

12*

for his immediate return. Whenever he received that envelope he would set out instantly, and would suffer no business to detain him. He often made marks in his letters to signify persons, and made Maggie do the same. Bearing in mind the possibility of his letters meeting other eyes, he mutilated several, tearing off portions he did not wish to be read. He at one time told her he would write in invisible ink, when the letters came open; but this was never done.

The morning of the day he sailed, October 11th, though noted as the 10th by his biographer, he came early to Twenty-second street. He had before spoken of having made his will, and said to Mrs. Fox that he had left a legacy "to that dear child." He said the same repeatedly to Margaret, and now again speaking of his will, added, "and you are well remembered in it." Margaret observed that the making of a will "was very sad;" but the Doctor, placing her drooping head upon his shoulder, explained that it was but a needful precaution on the eve of a journey.

The legacy he referred to was left in a "secret trust" to one of his brothers; the name of Miss Fox not appearing in his will. He had an excusable anxiety not to vex his family, while he wished her who had sacrificed for him her means of living, to enjoy what he was able to give her. This legacy was never paid, although the interest on it was paid for some time, under conditions never imposed by Dr. Kane. The offer of payment, if she would surrender

Dr. Kane's letters, has always been declined by his widow.

On this last morning, Dr. Kane had with him in the carriage the portrait of his beloved, painted by Fagnani, which had been his inseparable companion in his Arctic travels. He preferred carrying it with him to having it packed in a trunk. The ambrotype was finished, and had been left at Mrs. Fox's. It was to be copied in England by a celebrated artist.

The adieux were made, sad and tearful on both sides,—and the Doctor drove away to meet other friends. But neither friends, nor relatives, nor business, could prevent his returning to take another farewell just before the steamer sailed.

The final parting came. Again and again he clasped in his arms the poor girl whose love for him had been so patient and enduring, and was prized by him above all the world could bestow. With tears and sobs, tearing himself away, he bade her stand in the door, that he might see her till the carriage bore him out of sight. His weeping adieux were repeated many times after he left the door; then suddenly recollecting the ambrotype, he returned to the house for it, leaving the carriage at a little distance. Margaret walked with him back to the carriage. Even at this last moment he was tempted to give up his voyage. "It is for you to decide, Maggie!" he cried. "My passage is taken; but that is nothing. Tell me, shall I go, or stay?" This was repeated again and again, as it had been for days before. The Doctor was continually in the habit of asking her opinion, in this manner, upon every matter of importance to him.

But Margaret would not detain him.

Little did either think they would never meet again in this world.

———

The following note came from England from the Doctor:

[Dr. Kane to Mrs. Kane.]

"I have just time to catch the steamer, dear Tutie, to tell you of my safe arrival, and to beg you to write should you need anything. Pardon the haste of this letter, and believe me always as of old.

"I send you a ridiculous paragraph cut from a Liverpool paper."

———

The envelope containing the last note written by Dr. Kane to his Maggie, was directed in Mr. Grinnell's handwriting. The note was written on a leaf torn

out of his memorandum-book. The Doctor was so
feeble as to be unable to support himself, and could
only write a few words with difficulty. They were
the last words his hand ever traced to any human
being. His biographer says his latest letter was
addressed to Dr. S. W. Mitchell of Philadelphia, and
was dated November 15th—from London. This was
later, and was written on shipboard.

[Dr. Kane to Mrs. Kane.]

"DEAR TUTIE:—I am quite sick, and have gone
to Havana; only one week from New York. I have
received no letters from you; but write at once to E.
K. Kane, care of American Consul, Havana."

Margaret wrote in reply to the above:

[Mrs. Kane to Dr. Kane.]

"MY DEAR ELISHA:—Your welcome little note
was received this morning, for which I owe you
many thanks. I have heard of you often through the
newspapers.

"You can imagine my feelings when I heard that

your physicians had ordered you to go to St. Thomas; I only hope that you may soon recover.

"I would give worlds to see you, but can hardly expect to have that pleasure till May, as our climate is so awful for invalids.

"Mr. F. W. Wilson called here a few days since, and informed us that you had sailed in the Oriental for the West Indies, accompanied by your faithful friend Cornelius Grinnell.

"I am not happy when you are away.

"Could I only see you I would say much that I cannot write.

" In love yours faithfully,

" MARGARET.

"Dr. E. K. KANE.
  "Care of American Consul, Havana."

———

She wrote again some time afterwards:

"MY DEAR DR. KANE:—How are you? Why have you not written? or, if you were too ill to write, why have you not given Morton orders to do so? Had you attended to this it would have made me much happier. I always thought you were very wise; but, indeed, my powers of wisdom would have far surpassed yours.

"I know not whether this will find you alive or not; only think how very cruel it is in you to leave me to all manner of awful imaginings! I read the newspaper articles, of course; but what reliance can I place on what they say! One day they say that you are rapidly recovering, and perhaps the next morning the old Tribune will say,—'Dr. Kane is dangerously ill, and it is feared he will not live to return to his home again.' Oh, dear, I am so unhappy! Mr. Grinnell has returned, and I am sometimes tempted to ask Dr. Bayard to take me to his house, and see if he could give any satisfactory news concerning your health. But there it is;—I have been so very unkind to the poor fellow in sending so abruptly for my letters, that I would not dare go to him. Did the Consul hand you my letters? Are you Dr. Kane or not? Really, I begin to doubt that I have ever known Dr. Kane!

"I am very well, but wretchedly unhappy. Katie sends much love.

"From yours truly,
"MARGARET FOX."

"P. S.—Do write at once, or get Morton to write."

But the excitement caused by the letter preceding
this one had been almost too much for the enfeebled
frame of the sufferer, and this last was not given to
him.   He was paralysed and speechless before it
could reach him.

The cruel uncertainty felt by Margaret whether
her letter would ever meet the eyes of him for whom
it was written—the uncertainty into whose hands it
might fall, induced her to use the same signature she
had formerly used, though aware she was now entitled
to bear the name of him she loved.   It had been
agreed between them that the marriage should be
conceàled till May, from the knowledge of all but
those who had witnessed it; and Dr. Kane had especially charged her not to sign herself Kane, even
under cover to his brother.

Mrs. Fox and her daughter were making preparations to go to Havana, according to Dr. Kane's earnest
request before they parted, when they received the
news of his death.   This occurred on the 16th February, 1857.   Margaret read through the fatal paragraph in silence, though deadly pale; then turned to
leave the room, and dropped on the floor insensible.
No human thought could measure her sorrow.   An
illness of many months followed; and during the
greater part of the time she was shut up in a dark
room, utterly inconsolable, and unable to bear the
light of day.

The following fragment was penned by her more than two years afterwards:

"TO MY BELOVED.

" Oh, that I could die and be with thee! How can thy place be filled! How can my sorrow be alleviated? Thou art missed every moment more and more!

" No heart can ever be like thine—no voice so worshipped—no smile so loved! Alas! alas! never shall I again find in this weary world such love—such fidelity—such tenderness—as I received from my beloved! Oh, that I could die and be with thee!

"MARGARET.

"SEPTEMBER 17th, 1859."

A correspondent of the Evening Post thus writes of the great American Explorer—noticing Hicks's painting of him sitting in the cabin of the Advance:

" We look upon him here with his grasp of mind, its inspiration, the enthronement of genius and virtuous disinterestedness and worth. Here he sits in his hall of science, in the dim frozen regions where the keel of a navigator had never before penetrated; and at an hour when no human eye rested upon him, he is found in that temple of democracy in which he came to learn to confess his ignorance before the Great Supreme, and to find that it is only dignity of intellect, the largeness and fulness of knowledge, which confers superiority over man!

"Here he sits, smitten, as it were, suddenly with a craving for more mental illumination, whilst enjoying the highest of all pleasures, the perception of some fresh truth which will give a new standard to merit, and a new pursuit to men! Here he sits, in these trackless seas, the comprehensive thinker, the law-giver and founder of knowledge, opening a new vein of thought, and creating fresh science and power. Steadfast integrity, incorruptible courage, and heavenly benevolence are written upon his brow; but, with all his exalted humanity, we see in his face what Kent loved in Lear—'Authority.' Superior in morals, superior in intellect and in knowledge, it only needed his natural reticence to observe all circumstances, and to bring to bear at the right time all the faculties which he possessed, and which gave him what mankind concedes to him,—*greatness!*"

Add to "Authority"—Love—to complete the portrait.

Mrs. Kane felt convinced that the Doctor had left for her some word or message—some blessing with parting breath; and she was intensely anxious to know it. As soon as she was able to hold a pen, she wrote to one of the Doctor's brothers, in her former name—which she retained as a middle name—for she was careful to avoid wounding the pride of the family, and felt no disposition to intrude on them the relation in which she stood to them.

[Mrs. Kane to Mr. Kane.]

"MY DEAR MR. KANE:—I know the Doctor must have left some message for me, and know that you will not refuse to deliver it, even though it gives you much pain in recalling the name of him whose memory is and ever will be sacred. I have always held a religious faith in the deep sincerity of the Doctor's love, and his memory will always remain a beautiful green in my unchanged affections.

"'I can never realize that he is gone—gone for ever. Only seven months ago I bade him farewell, here, in this very room, only an hour before his departure for England, and little thought that it would be the last, long farewell.

"With my kindest regards, believe me,

"Sincerely yours,

"MARGARET FOX.

"EAST TWENTY-SECOND ST."

She said well in the expression "religious faith;" her devotion was indeed a religion to her. She lived, and has ever since lived, alone in the memory of her beloved. It has been "a love repressing all other life in her heart." That "life-warm correspondence" seems to have drained the vitality of her being. No worldly allurement, no attraction of society, no solicitation of friends, could or can draw her from continual, unceasing thoughts of him. One room, containing his letters and various gifts, where hang his portrait and the map of his wanderings,—is her favorite resort, and is kept as a sanctuary. Her opinions of persons and views of things are moulded entirely by her recollections of his. His hatred of spiritualism is her abiding feeling in regard to it, and she shuns its votaries. Her former friends, even her kindred, except her parents and the sister whom the Doctor liked, are as aliens and strangers. "Would dear Elisha like me to do this?"—is the test by which she regulates conduct at all times and under all circumstances. Never was widow's heart more entirely buried in the grave of the lost one. What her love may have wanted in passion, is made up in constancy; a constancy none of life's scenes can dim or enfeeble; a constancy that will endure to death.

In August, 1858, she became a member of the Roman Catholic Church. Dr. Kane had often advised her to join this church, and many times had accompanied her to vespers at St. Anne's, in Eighth street,

New York. The ceremony of her baptism, at St. Peter's Church, in Barclay street, New York, was new in this country, and was attended by a large assemblage. The lady was attired in white, and was accompanied by her sponsors, her father and mother, and her youngest sister. The priest made the sign of the cross upon the candidate's forehead, ears, eyes, nose and mouth, breast and shoulders, repeating appropriate words in Latin. She was anointed with the holy oils, and introduced into the church by receiving the stole, a long white veil reaching to the ground, and a burning light, emblematic of the faith. The occasion was the Feast of the Assumption, and the church and altar were decorated, the statue of the Virgin being covered with flowers.

One of the New York papers, describing the ceremony, remarked concerning the new convert:—

"She is a very interesting and lovely young lady, and is very young. She has large dark Madonna eyes, a sweet expressive mouth, a petite and delicately moulded form, and a regal carriage of the head, with an aristocratic air quite uncommon. Miss Fox, it is said, was placed at school in Philadelphia by the lamented Kane, the Arctic voyager, who loved her as a sister, and whose brotherly interest in the fair girl was dearly cherished even in his last moments."

———

Governor Tallmadge wrote to Mrs. Kane as follows, on reading the account of this baptism :—

"SARATOGA SPRINGS, August 17th, 1858.

" MY DEAR MAGGIE :—I saw in the Herald of yesterday an account of your connecting yourself with the Roman Catholic Church. I most sincerely hope it will add to your comfort and happiness. I know how depressed and disconsolate you have been since your disappointment in a matter of the heart, to which we all look forward for happiness in this life. But remember, my dear young friend, that our trials and disappointments here are but for a brief season, and that we shall again meet those we have loved, where there shall be no separation for ever.

" I am here for a time to get rid of a partial return of my bronchial difficulty. I have had it three times removed by a mercurial treatment ; I wish to avoid that remedy if I can. I am improving, and hope in due time to be entirely relieved.

"I hope your health is improving. I regretted I could not see you when I was last in New York. I wished to visit New York once more before I returned home; but my doctor advised me to avoid your *salt* atmosphere. Be so kind as to write me a line, however brief, whilst I remain here. Direct ' U. S. Hotel, Saratoga Springs.'

"Remember me most kindly to your mother and Katy, and believe me always,

"Most affectionately

"Your sincere friend,

"N. P. TALLMADGE."

———

Six months later the Governor sent her another letter of condolence:

"LITHGOW, DUTCHESS COUNTY, N. Y.
"March 10th, 1859.

"MY DEAR MAGGIE:—I was very much gratified in the receipt of your very kind letter of yesterday. I truly sympathize with you, my young friend, in all your cares and sorrows. I appreciate your feelings when contemplating 'the loved and lost,' and I am rejoiced that in your contemplations of the future ' all seems bright and beautiful.' Thus it shall ever be.

Your pure and Christian life will assure you a blissful and happy future, and you will enjoy the companionship of the 'loved one' gone before you, to be no more separated for ever. How consoling the thought! How heart-cheering the contemplation! Why, then, mourn over the present separation? It is but for a brief season. No, my young friend, you should be happy in the contemplation of your future happiness. Besides, it is a duty we all owe, to be cheerful for the sake of friends around us; whilst, at the same time, it contributes to our own happiness. The longer we continue here in works of love to God and our neighbor, the better we shall be prepared to enter upon an elevated plane hereafter, and to commence a course of everlasting progression. Let us, therefore, dissipate the shadows here in anticipation of the sunshine hereafter. I shall take great pleasure in talking with you on this subject when I meet you.

"I cannot tell how soon I can see you. My cough is better; but my doctor is unwilling to have me exposed to the severe March winds, and I am somewhat afraid of the salt air of New York in the present state of my respiratory organs.

"Remember me kindly to your mother and Katy, and believe me

"Your sincere and devoted friend,
"N. P. TALLMADGE."

THE END.

www.ingramcontent.com/pod-product-compliance
Ingram Content Group UK Ltd.
Pitfield, Milton Keynes, MK11 3LW, UK
UKHW042154280225
455719UK00001B/330